Roman Military Stone-built Granaries in Britain

Anne P. Gentry

British Archaeological Reports 32
1976

British Archaeological Reports
122 Banbury Road, Oxford OX2 7BP, England

GENERAL EDITORS

A.C.C. Brodr bb, M.A.   A.R. Hands, B.Sc., M.A., D.Phil.
Mrs. Y.M. Hands   D.R. Walker, M.A.

ADVISORY EDITORS

C.B. Burgess, M.A.   Neil Cossons, M.A., F.S.A., F.M.A.
Professor B.W. Cunliffe, M.A., Ph.D., F.S.A.
Sonia Chadwick Hawkes, B.A., M.A., F.S.A.
Professor G.D.B. Jones, M.A., D.Phil., F.S.A.
Frances Lynch, M.A., F.S.A.   P.A. Mellars, M.A., Ph.D.
P.A. Rahtz, M.A., F.S.A.

B.A.R. 32, 1976: "Roman Military Stone-Built Granaries in Britain"
© Anne P. Gentry, 1976

The author's moral rights under the 1988 UK Copyright,
Designs and Patents Act are hereby expressly asserted.

All rights reserved. No part of this work may be copied, reproduced, stored, sold, distributed, scanned, saved in any form of digital format or transmitted in any form digitally, without the written permission of the Publisher.

ISBN 9780904531459 paperback
ISBN 9781407319674 e-book
DOI https://doi.org/10.30861/9780904531459
A catalogue record for this book is available from the British Library
This book is available at www.barpublishing.com

ROMAN MILITARY STONE-BUILT GRANARIES IN BRITAIN

CONTENTS

Page

Acknowledgements

List of Figures

List of Plates, Tables and Maps

Abbreviations

Bibliography

PART I

1.	Introduction	1
2.	Principles and Problems of Grain Storage	2
3.	Classical references to Grain Storage	5
4.	Comparison of excavated structures	7
5.	Structural aspects, and their interpretation	15
6.	Provisioning of Roman Forts and the Capacity of Granaries	23
7.	Appendices	35
8.	Index	47

PART II

Catalogue of excavated examples — 49

1.	Introduction	51
2.	Location of sites discussed	52
3.	Comparison of external wall and buttress dimensions	55
4.	Catalogue	57

ACKNOWLEDGEMENTS

This work is based upon an undergraduate thesis submitted to the University of Wales in 1975.

I am greatly indebted to Dr. M. G. Jarrett for his advice and encouragement. He has very kindly provided details of garrisons and related inscriptions for each catalogue entry and has also read and criticised an earlier draft of the text.

I should like to thank Mr. G. Boon of the Department of Archaeology, National Museum of Wales, for his help and for making provision for me to examine and weigh a selection of roofing tiles from Caerleon. Also, Dr. W. H. Manning with whom I have discussed several points.

Mr. W. R. Davies of the Department of Civil Engineering, U.W.I.S.T. and my father Mr. P. W. H. Gentry gave valuable assistance in the preparation of the section upon structural requirements. In this connection I am also extremely grateful to Mr. James Simpson for his considerable help in compiling this data and for checking the calculations in the appendices.

I am grateful for the help given by Mr. R. W. Howe of the Pest Infestation Control Laboratory, with whom I have communicated on a number of points. Mr. T. Compton undertook the photographic reduction of my plans. Also Mr. A. E. Johnson drew the possible granary reconstruction and that of the tiled roof and also contributed much advice and constructive criticism.

I am also indebted to Mr. J. P. Gillam who has very generously allowed me access to material on the granaries at Corbridge in advance of his own publication, and to Dr. D. J. Breeze for providing information on his recent excavations at Bearsden.

Finally I should like to thank Professor G. D. B. Jones for his helpful comments on the original text.

LIST OF FIGURES

		Page
1.	Suggested reconstruction	17
2.	Tiled roof: suggested construction	19
3.	South Shields: Severan Supply Base	21
4.	Grain distribution model	29
5.	Granary floor area as a percentage of fort area	31
6.	Granary plans: Ambleside, Balmuildy, Bar Hill, Benwell, Birrens	61
7.	Granary plans: Brecon Gaer, Brough on Noe, Cadder, Caerhun, Caernarfon, Caersws II	65
8.	Granary plans: Camelon, Cappuck, Castell Collen, Castlecary, Castledykes, Chester-le-Street, Chester (3)	69
9.	Granary plans: Corbridge. Structural Phases	73
10.	Granary plans: Chesters, Cramond, Crawford II, Croy Hill, Drumburgh, Gelligaer II	79
11.	Granary plans: Greatchesters, Haltwhistle Burn, Hardknott, High Rochester, Housesteads, Ilkley	83
12.	Granary plans: Lyne, Mumrills, Newstead	87
13.	Granary plans: Old Church, Brampton, Old Kilpatrick, Penydarren, Ribchester, Rudchester	91
14.	Granary plans: Rough Castle, Slack, South Shields, Templeborough	93

LIST OF PLATES

IA   Corbridge: west granary
B   Corbridge (west). Longitudinal sleeper walls supporting flagged floor

IIA   Corbridge (east). Ventilator with central mullion
B   Corbridge (east). Loading platform, portico column, and drain

IIIA   Housesteads (north). Pillar floor supports
B   Housesteads (north). Relationship of ventilator to floor supports

TABLES

1.	Granary floor area expressed as a proportion of the total internal fort area	30
2.	Comparison of granary floor area, presumed garrison and theoretical annual grain requirement	32
3.	Comparison of fort area, granary floor area and garrison requirements relating to timber granaries	34
4.	Dimensions of external walls and buttresses	55

MAPS

1.	The location of granaries studied	53
2.	Northern Britain	54

ABBREVIATIONS

AA, 1-4	Archaeologia Aeliana, 1st to 4th series. Society of Antiquaries of Newcastle upon Tyne.
Ant. J.	The Antiquaries Journal, London.
Arch. Camb.	Archaeologia Cambrensis, Cardiff.
Arch. J.	Archaeological Journal, London.
AW	Archaeology in Wales, Cardiff.
BAR	British Archaeological Reports, Oxford.
BBCS	Bulletin of the Board of Celtic Studies, Cardiff.
Brit.	Britannia, London.
Bull. Ent. Res.	Bulletin of Entymological Research.
Carm. Antiq.	The Carmarthen Antiquary, Carmarthen.
CIL	Corpus Inscriptionum Latinarum.
Curr. Arch.	Current Archaeology.
CW, 1-2	Transactions of the Cumberland and Westmorland Antiquarian and Archaeological Society, Carlisle.
Derb. Arch. J.	Derbyshire Archaeological Journal.
Dur. Univ. Gaz.	Durham University Gazette.
J. Agric. Eng. Res.	Journal of Agricultural Engineering and Research.
J. Chester. Arch. Soc.	Journal of the Architectural, Archaeological and Historic Society ... of Chester.
JRS	Journal of Roman Studies, London.
Kent Arch. Rev.	Kent Archaeological Review.
Mont. Coll.	Collections ... pertaining to Montgomeryshire, Welshpool
New Phyt.	New Phytologist.
PPS	Proceedings of the Prehistoric Society.
PSAS	Proceedings of the Society of Antiquaries of Scotland, Edinburgh.
RIB	Collingwood, R. G. and Wright, R. P. <u>The Roman Inscriptions of Britain</u>, 1. Oxford 1965.

Saal. J.	Saalburg Jahrbuch, Berlin.
TBGAS	Transactions of the Bristol and Gloucestershire Archaeological Society.
Trans. Birm. Arch. Soc.	Transactions of the Birmingham Archaeological Society.
VCH	Victoria History of the Counties of England.
YAJ	Yorkshire Archaeological Journal

BIBLIOGRAPHY

Classical References

Marcus Porcius Cato	De Agricultura
Cicero	In Verr.
Columella	De Re Rustica
Herodian	
Pliny	Naturalis Historia
Polybius	The Histories
SHA	Scriptores Historiae Augustae
	Hadrianus
Tacitus	Agricola
Marcus Terentius Varro	Res Rusticae
Vitruvius	De Architectura

Bibliography for granaries

Birley, E, 1938: Excavations at Birrens, 1936-7, PSAS LXXII (1937-8), 280.

Birley, E, 1960: Chesters Roman Fort, Ministry of Works Guide (1960).

Bosanquet, R. C., 1904: Excavations at Housesteads Roman Fort, AA2 XXV, (1904), 235.

Breeze, D. J., 1968: Excavations at South Shields 1966 and 1967, Archaeological Newsbulletin No. 50 (April 1968).

Brewis, J. Parker, 1924: Roman Rudchester. Report on Excavations, 1924, AA4 1 (1925), 99.

Bruce, J. Collingwood, 1857: Excavations at Bremenium AA 2 1, (1857), 76.

Bruce, J. Collingwood, 1860: Excavations at Birdoswald AA 2 IV, (1860), 249.

Buchanan, M., 1900: An account of the Excavation of the Roman station of Camelon, near Falkirk, Stirlingshire, PSAS XXXV, (1900), 365.

Buchanan, M., 1903: Excavation of Castlecary fort on the Antonine Vallum, PSAS XXXVII, (1903), 308.

Buchanan, M., 1905: Report on the Society's excavation of Rough Castle on the Antonine Vallum, PSAS XXXIX, (1905), 474.

Buckland, P. C. and Dolby, M. J., 1972: Doncaster, <u>Curr. Arch.</u> (1971-2), 274.

Buckland, P. C. and Dolby, M. J., 1973: note in <u>Brit.</u> IV, (1973), 282.

Charlesworth, D., 1963: The Granaries at Hardknott Castle, <u>CW</u> 2, LXIII (1963), 148-152.

Christison, D., 1895: An account of the Excavation of Birrens, a Roman station in Annandale, <u>PSAS</u> XXX, (1895-6), 112.

Christison, D., 1901: Excavation of the Roman Camp at Lyne, Peebleshire, <u>PSAS</u> XXXV, (1901), 180.

Clarke, J., 1933: <u>The Roman Fort at Cadder,</u> Glasgow, 1933.

Collingwood, R. G., 1915: The Exploration of the Roman Fort at Ambleside, <u>CW</u> 2, XV (1915), 24.

Collingwood, R. G., 1928: Hardknot Castle, <u>CW 2</u>, XXVIII (1928), 329.

Collingwood, R. G., 1933: Bruce, J. C. <u>Handbook to the Roman Wall,</u> 9th ed. by Collingwood, Newcastle upon Tyne, 1933.

Curle, J., 1911: <u>Newstead: A Roman Frontier Post and its People,</u> Glasgow, 1911, 58.

Daniels, C. M., Jones, G. D. B. and Putnam, W. G., 1966: <u>Mont Coll.</u> 59 (1965-6), 112-5.

<u>Daniels et al.,</u> 1967: <u>Mont Coll.</u> 60 (1966-7).

Dodd, P. W. and Woodward, A. M., 1923: Excavations at Slack, 1913-15, <u>Y.A.J.,</u> 26 (1920-3), 21.

Evelyn-White, H. G., 1914: Excavations at Castell Collen, Llandridnod Wells, <u>Arch. Camb.</u> 69 (= <u>Arch. Camb.</u> 6.14, 1914), 19.

Forster, R. H. and Knowles, W. H., 1909: Corstopitum: Report on the excavations, <u>AA</u> 3 V, (1909), 314.

Forster, R. H. and Knowles, W. H., 1910: Corstopitum: Report on the excavations, <u>AA3</u> VI, (1910), 209-13.

Forster, R. H., 1912: <u>Corstopitum, a brief report on the Excavations from 1906-1911.</u> 1912.

Forster, R. H. and Knowles, W. H., 1915: Corstopitum: Report on the excavations, <u>AA</u> 3 XII (1915), 227.

Frere, S. S. and St. Joseph, J. K. S., 1974: The Roman Fortress at Longthorpe, <u>Brit.</u> V, (1974), 1-38.

Gibson, J. P., 1903: Excavations at Aesica, Great Chesters, <u>AA</u> 2 XXIV, (1903), 33.

Gibson, J. P. and Simpson, F. G., 1909: Excavations at Haltwhistle Burn, <u>AA</u> 3 V, (1909), 250.

Gillam, J. P., 1961a: Excavations at Haltonchesters, <u>Dur. Univ. Gaz.,</u> (1961), 6.

Gillam, J. P., 1961b: note in <u>JRS</u> 51, (1961), 164.

Gillam, J. P., 1962: note in JRS 52, (1962), 164.

Gillam, J. P., 1967: note in JRS 57, (1967), 177-8.

Gillam, J. P. and Tait, J. 1968: The Roman Fort at Chester-le-Street, AA 4 XLVI, (1968), 75-96.

Gillam, J. P. and Tait, J., 1971: The Investigation of the Commander's House Area, on Site XI, Corbridge, 1958-70; The Structures, AA 4 XLIX, (1971), 1-28.

Hartley, B. R., 1958: note in JRS 48, (1958), 135.

Hartley, B. R., 1966: Proc. Leeds Philosophical and Literary Soc., xii, (1966), 23-72.

Hartley, K. F., 1972: note in Brit. II, (1972), 254.

Haverfield, F., 1899: Excavations at Drumburgh, CW 1 XVI, (1899), 81.

H.M.S.O., 1967: RCHM (Scotland), Peeblesshire I. H.M.S.O. 1967, 172-5.

Hobley, B., 1969 & 1972: Neronian-Vespasianic Military site at The Lunt, Baginton, Warwicks., Trans. Birm. Arch. Soc. 83, (1969), 65-129 and 85, (1972), 8-92.

Hogg, A. H. A., 1968: Pen Llystyn: A Roman Fort and Other Remains, Arch. J. 125, (1968), 101-93.

Hopkinson, J., 1928: The Roman Fort at Ribchester, 3rd edition by Atkinson, D., Manchester, 1928, 14.

James, F. T., 1906: Roman remains: Penydarren Park, Merthyr Tydfil, Arch. Camb. 61, (= Arch. Camb. 6, 1906), 193-208.

Jarrett, M. G., 1968a: The Roman Fort at Brecon Gaer: some problems, BBCS 22, (1966-8), 426-32.

Jones, G. D. B. and Birley, A. R., 1966: note in JRS LVI, (1966), 196.

Jones, G. D. B. and Wild, J. P., 1967-9: Manchester University Excavations at Brough on Noe, Derb. Arch. J. LXXXVII and LXXXIX (1967-9).

Jones, G. D. B. et al., 1972: note in AW (1972), 23-4.

Jones, G. D. B. et al., 1973: note in Brit. IV, (1973), 272.

Jones, G. D. B. and Little, J. H., 1973: Excavations on the Roman Fort at Pumpsaint, Carmarthenshire: Interim Report 1972. Carm. Antiq. (1973), 3-21.

Macdonald, G., 1906: Roman Forts on the Bar Hill, Glasgow, 1906, 40.

Macdonald, G. and Curle, A., 1928: The Roman Fort at Mumrills, near Falkirk, PSAS LXIII, (1928), 431.

Macdonald, G., 1937: A further note on the Roman Fort at Croy Hill, PSAS LXXI, (1936-7), 56.

Manning, W.H., 1974: Excavations in the Roman Fortress at Usk, Monmouthshire, Roman Frontier Studies 1969. ed. Birley, E., Dobson, B. and Jarrett, M. G., (1974), 61-9.

Maxwell, G., 1972: Excavations at the Roman fort of Crawford, Lanarkshire, PSAS 104, (1971-2), 147-200.

May, R., 1922: The Roman Forts of Templeborough near Rotherham, Rotherham, 1922, 39.

Miller, S. N., 1922: Roman Fort at Balmuildy, Glasgow, 1922, 26.

Miller, S. N., 1928: Roman Fort at Old Kilpatrick, Glasgow, 1928, 21.

Ministry of Works, 1952: Guide to the Roman Fort at Housesteads, ed. Birley, E., 1952.

Norman, H., 1859: Excavations at Birdoswald, AA 2 IV, (1859), 249.

Petch, D. F. and Thompson, F. H., 1959: Excavations in Commonhall St., Chester, 1954-6: The Granaries of the Legionary Fortress of Deva, Chester Arch. Soc. J. XLVI, (1959), 33-60.

Philp, B., 1971: The Classis Britannica and Saxon Shore Forts at Dover - an interim report, Kent Arch. Rev. 23 (1971).

Philp, B., 1972: The Dover Roman Forts, Kent Arch. Rev. 28 (1972).

Pryce, F. N., 1940: Mont. Coll. 46 (1940), 67 ff.

Rae, A., 1959-62: notes in JRS 49 (1959), 104; JRS 51 (1961), 161; and JRS 52 (1962), 163.

Rae, A. and V., 1974: The Roman Fort at Cramond, Brit. V, (1974), 165.

Reynolds, P. K. Bailie, 1938: Excavations on the site of the Roman fort of Kanovium at Caerhun, Caernarvonshire, Cardiff, 1938.

Richmond, I. A., 1934: The Roman Fort at South Shields, AA 4 XI (1934), 92.

Richmond, I.A. and McIntyre, J., 1939: The Agricolan Fort at Fendoch, PSAS LXXIII, (1938-9), 110-154.

Richmond, I. A., 1940: The Romans in Redesdale, NCH XV, (1940), 63 ff.

   1941: note in JRS 31, (1941), 129.

   1947: note in JRS 37, (1947), 165.

   1948: note in JRS 38, (1948), 82.

   1950: Newstead, PSAS LXXXIV, (1949-50), 19.

Richmond, I.A. and Gillam, J. P., 1950: Excavations on the Roman Site at Corbridge, 1946-9 AA 4 XXVIII, (1950), 152-201.

Richmond, I. A., 1959: note in JRS 49, (1959), 106-7.

   1961: note in JRS 51, (1961), 158.

Robertson, A. S., 1964: The Roman Fort at Castledykes, Edinburgh and London, 1964.

Robertson, A. S., 1975: Birrens (Blatobulgium), Edinburgh, 1975.

Robertson, A. S., Scott, M. and Keppie, L., 1975: Bar Hill: A Roman Fort and its Finds, BAR 16 (1975).

Shaw, N., Smith, D. J. and Gillam. J. P., 1958: note in JRS 48, (1958).

Sheffield University, 1959: note in JRS 49, (1959), 108.

Simpson, F. G. and Richmond, I. A., 1931: Excavations on Hadrian's Wall in the Birdoswald-Pike Hill Sector, 1930, CW 2 XXXI, (1931), 122-34.

Simpson, F. G. and Richmond, I. A., 1936: The Roman Fort on the Stanegate, and other remains, at Old Church, Brampton, CW 2 XXXVI. (1936), 174.

Simpson, F. G. and Richmond, I. A., 1941: The Roman Fort on Hadrian's Wall at Benwell, AA 4 XIX, (1941), 17.

Simpson, F. G. and Richmond, I. A., 1952: The Roman Fort at Drumburgh, CW 2 LII, (1952), 9.

Stevenson, G. H. and Miller, S. N., 1912: Report on the Excavations at the Roman Fort of Cappuck, Roxburghshire, PSAS XLVI (1912), 458.

St. Joseph, J. K. S., 1951: Air reconnaissance of Northern Britain, JRS 41, (1951), 52-65.

St. Joseph, J. K. S., 1961: Air reconnaissance in Britain 1958-60, JRS 51, (1961), 124.

Wade, W. V., 1952: note in JRS 42, (1952), 91.

Ward, J., 1903: The Roman Fort of Gellygaer, London, 1903.

Wheeler, R. E. M., 1922: The Segontium Excavations, 1922, Arch. Camb. LXXVII, (= Arch. Camb. 7, 2.1922), 302.

Wheeler, R. E. M., 1924: Segontium and the Roman occupation of Wales, 1924.

Wheeler, R. E. M., 1926 a: Excavations at Brecon Gaer, Y Cymmrodor, XXXVII, (1926).

Wheeler, R. E. M., 1926 b: Roman Fort near Brecon, 1926.

Woodward, A. M., 1926: The Roman Fort at Ilkley, Y.A.J. 28 (1924-6), 184.

General

Armstrong, M. T. and Howe, R. W., 1963: The saw-toothed Grain Beetle Oryzaephilus surinamensis, in home grown grain, J. Agric. Eng. Res. 8 No. 3, (1963), 256-261.

Birley, E., 1953: Roman Britain and the Roman Army, Kendal, 1953.

Birley, E., 1961: Research on Hadrian's Wall, Kendal, 1961.

Boon, G., 1974: Silchester, 1974.

Booth, L. G. and Reece, P. O., 1967: The Structural Use of Timber, 1967.

Brassington, M., 1975: A Reappraisal of the Western Enclave and Environs, Corstopitum, Brit. VI, (1975), 62-75.

Breeze, D. and Dobson, B., 1969: Fort types on Hadrian's Wall, AA 4 XLVII, (1969), 15.

Breeze, D. and Dobson, B., 1973: The Development of the Mural Frontier in Britain from Hadrian to Caracalla, PSAS 102, (1969-70), 109-21.

Breeze, D. and Dobson, B., 1974: Fort Types as a Guide to Garrisons: a Reconsideration, Roman Frontier Studies 1969, (1974), ed. Birley, E., Dobson, B. and Jarrett, M. G.

Bulmer, W., 1969: The Provisioning of Roman Forts: A reappraisal of ration storage, AA 4 XLVII. (1969).

Bulmer, W., 1972: Review of Rickman's Roman Granaries and Store-buildings, JRS 62, (1972), 205-6.

Collingwood, R. G. and Richmond, I. A., 1971: The Archaeology of Roman Britain, revised 1971.

Coombs, C. W. and Freeman, J. A., 1955: The insect fauna of an Empty Granary, Bull. Ent. Res. 46, (1955), 399-417.

Coope, G. R. and Osborne, P. J., 1967: Report on the Coleopterous Fauna of the Roman well at Barnsley Park, Gloucestershire, TBGAS 86, (1967).

Crawford, O. G. S., 1949: Topography of Roman Scotland North of the Antonine Wall, 1949.

Davey, N., 1961: A History of Building Materials, London, 1961.

Davies, R. W., 1971: The Roman Military Diet, Brit. II, (1971).

Fink, R. O., 1971: Roman Military Records on Papyrus, 1971.

Frere, S. S., 1967: Britannia, 1967.

Fryer, J., 1973: The harbour installations of Roman Britain, Marine Archaeology, (Colston Papers), ed. Blackman, D. J., 1973.

Haverfield, F., 1916: Modius Claytonensis: the Roman Bronze Measure from Carvoran, AA 3 XIII, (1916).

Haverfield, F. and Collingwood, R. G., 1920: The Provisioning of Roman Forts, CW 2 XX, (1920).

Helbaek, H., 1952: Early crops in Southern England, PPS 18, (1952), 194.

Helbaek, H., 1964: The Isca Grain, a Roman plant introduction in Britain, New Phyt. 63, (1964), 158.

Hinton, H. E. and Corbet, A. S., 1972: Common Insect Pests of Stored Food Products, British Museum (Natural History), 1972.

H.M.S.O., 1966: Farm Grain Drying and Storage, Ministry of Ag. Fish and Food, Bulletin No. 149, 1966.

H.M.S.O., 1971: Farm Buildings, Ministry of Ag. Fish and Food, 1971.

Holt, J. and Nix, J. S., 1961: Safe in store, Farmer and Stockbreeder, 9-5-61.

Jacobi, H. von, 1914: Römische Getreidemühlen, Saal. J. III, (1912), 75-95.

Jarrett, M. G., 1968: Legio XX Valeria Victrix in Britain, Arch. Camb. 117, (1968), 77-91.

Jasny, N., 1944: Wheat Prices and Milling Costs in Classical Rome, Wheat Studies of the Food Research Institute, Vol. XX No. 4, (March 1944), Stanford University, California, 137-170.

Macdonald, G., 1934: The Roman Wall in Scotland, 2nd edition, 1934.

Manning, W. H., 1975: Roman Military Timber Granaries in Britain, Saal. J. XXXII, (1975), 105-129.

McKay, W. B., 1971: Building Construction, I and II, 1971.

Miller, S. N. (ed.) 1952: The Roman Occupation of south-west Scotland, Glasgow, 1952.

Monte, G. dal 1956: La presenza di insetti dei granari in frumento negli scari di ercolano, Redia, 41, (1956), 23-8.

Moritz, L. A., 1958: Grain Mills and Flour in Classical Antiquity, Oxford, 1958.

Morley, A., 1953: Strength of Materials, 1953.

Nash-Williams, V. E., 1959: The Roman Frontier in Wales, Cardiff, 1969 2nd revised edition by Michael G. Jarrett.

Nix, J. S., 1956: Drying and storing grain on the farm, University of Cambridge, Farm Economics Branch Report, 44, 1956.

O'Neill, H., 1965: Stone for Building, 1965.

Osborne, P. J., 1971: An insect fauna from the Roman site at Alcester, Warwickshire, Brit. II, (1971), 156-165.

Oxley, T. A., 1948: The Scientific Principles of Grain Storage, Liverpool, 1948.

Petrikovits, H. von: Die Innenbauten römischer Legionslager während der Prinzipatszeit, 1974.

Rich, A., 1901: A Dictionary of Roman and Greek Antiquities, 1901.

Rickman, G. E., 1971: Roman Granaries and Storebuildings, Cambridge, 1971.

Singer, C. et al., 1956: A History of Technology, II, Oxford, 1956.

Simpson, G., 1964: Britons and the Roman Army, London, 1964.

Smith, W., 1849: Dictionary of Greek and Roman Antiquities, 1849.

Solomon, M. E. and Adamson, B. E., 1955: The powers of survival of storage and domestic pests under winter conditions in Britain, Bull. Ent. Res. 46, (1955), 311-355.

Thompson, F. H., 1965: Roman Cheshire, Chester, 1965.

Ward, J., 1911: Romano-British Buildings and Earthworks, London.

Watson, G. R., 1969: *The Roman Soldier*, 1969.

Webster, G., 1969: *The Roman Imperial Army*, London, 1969.

Weller, J. B., 1965: *Farm Buildings*, I, London, 1965.

Wilkes, J. J., 1965: Early Fourth-century rebuilding in Hadrian's Wall Forts, from *Britain and Rome*, ed. Jarrett, M. G. and Dobson, B., 1965.

INTRODUCTION

The identification and location of the granaries (horrea) within Roman forts has seldom presented any real problems to their excavators. In the past, the tendency has been to cut sections through the defences of a recognised Roman fort, locate the gateways, and to concentrate attention upon the central buildings. The principia always occupied the centre of the fort, fronting onto the main thoroughfare (via principalis), and the granaries were almost invariably situated on one or both sides of it, within the central range.

From the beginning of the 2nd century A.D. forts began to be rebuilt or constructed de novo in stone. The most likely candidates for masonry construction were these central buildings, and even in forts where the timber barracks were never replaced in stone the principia and horrea were frequently stone-built and substantial. The distinctive ground plan of these buildings; the courtyard plan of the principia and the thick walled, heavily buttressed granary make them easily recognisable.

It is for these reasons that so many granaries have been uncovered by nineteenth and early twentieth century excavators. Nevertheless they still present problems to the modern archaeologist. A large proportion of the granaries included in this study were excavated more than half a century ago, at a time before the introduction of many modern techniques, when often the principal method of excavation was to locate one wall and simply follow it round to produce a plan. The interior may have been examined completely, or may have been subjected to the digging of a diagonal trench across the building in the hope of detecting any internal features. Many details concerning the construction of individual granaries have thus been inadequately recorded. In addition, from the excavation reports it is often difficult to pinpoint a date for the granary because the main preoccupation was usually with the periods of occupation of the fort as an entity rather than charting the history of individual structures within.

It is the purpose of this study to correlate all the available information concerning structural details and individual characteristics of the granaries so far excavated, and also to record others which as yet have only been located from the air. No attempt has been made here to trace the architectural traditions of the stone granary, as this subject has been extensively covered elsewhere.[1] Nor does the work include consideration of timber military granaries in Britain, as they have recently been the subject of a comprehensive survey.[2] Consideration has been given to the ideas on grain storage expressed by contemporary Roman writers. Also a section has been devoted purely to the problems of grain storage in general, whether in the Roman or modern world, with regard to such factors as temperature control, granary pests etc., factors which determined the design of many distinguishable features of the Roman military stone-built granary.

2. PRINCIPLES AND PROBLEMS OF GRAIN STORAGE
FAVOURABLE CONDITIONS FOR STORAGE

Grain continues to respire, taking in oxygen and giving off heat, carbon dioxide and water after it has been harvested. In order to preserve it in storage for later consumption it is necessary to slow down these processes as much as possible. The principal methods in effecting this retardation are to reduce the temperature, the moisture content, and the amount of oxygen available. A major problem in the bulk storage of grain is its susceptibility to infestation by bacteria, moulds, fungi and insects. The grain will remain dormant providing that the temperature and moisture content remain low, but if it is placed in storage whilst too hot or wet it will begin to germinate and the dampness will encourage the activity of bacteria in the surrounding air, resulting in the growth of moulds and fungi which cause it to rot. Reduction of the temperature and moisture content will serve to minimise this activity.

Three principal methods are used in modern practice; the cooling of dry grain to a temperature of less than $17.25^{\circ}C$ using air blown through ducts on or below the floor by electric fans, the refrigeration of damp grain at $0-7.5^{\circ}C$ or the exclusion of oxygen by storage in airtight silos.

Insect infestation damages the grain both directly, by eating or contaminating the cereal grains, and indirectly by causing heating of the grain, resulting in deterioration. Initially heating occurs in localised centres, 'hot spots' which gradually merge, increasing the temperature to as much as $43^{\circ}C$. The loss of moisture from these areas as the heating intensifies causes it to condense on the outer, cooler areas of the grain and encourages the onset of fungal growth. If unchecked this activity will render the grain unfit for either flour or malting.

The main species of insects and mites which occur in granaries today are the saw-toothed grain beetle (Oryzaephilus surinamensis (L.)); grain weevil (Sitophilus granarius (L.)); rust red grain beetle (Cryptolestes ferrugineus (Steph.)); and the flour mite (Acarus Siro (L.)). It has been generally believed that the saw-toothed grain beetle was a relatively modern introduction to Britain caused by the increase in commercial traffic. However, analysis of insect fauna from two sites has revealed its presence in Roman Britain. The saw-toothed grain beetle was found in a well sealed by 4th century building rubble at Barnsley Park, Gloucestershire, and a late 2nd century rubbish pit at Alcester, Warwickshire has revealed evidence for twenty individuals in association with four other pests of stored foods; Sitophilus granarius, Stegobium paniceum, Palorus subdepressus and Tenebrio obscurus.[3]

The grain weevil bores holes into the cereal grains and deposits eggs in them which hatch into larvae and feed upon the flour; it is usually associated with wheat and barley, and perhaps rye. The saw-toothed grain beetle cannot attack undamaged cereals and can only survive after initial weevil damage, or in grain which includes broken seeds and dust.[4] Competition between the various species is dependent upon moisture and temperature conditions. For example, the grain weevil needs 15°C to develop and a moisture content of 11%, whereas the saw-toothed grain beetle needs 20°C to become active, but can withstand drier conditions. In favourable conditions they can breed and develop extremely rapidly.

To prevent the growth of these insects and also moulds and bacteria the moisture content of the grain must be reduced. To prevent any growth it would be necessary to reduce it to 8-10%, but this is not generally practical in a modern storage unit, still less in its Roman counterpart. In order to store grain successfully either in bulk or in closely stacked sacks, without turning it over or introducing any forced ventilation, for a period of nine months to a year, the maximum moisture content possible is 14% at 15.6°C. As the moisture of the grain increases, so the temperature necessary to prevent it from insect activity must decrease.

Temperature is very closely linked with moisture content in regard to insect growth. It is necessary to store grain below a temperature of 15.6°C to eliminate insect activity, but to prevent mould and bacteria growth it must be further decreased according to moisture content. A minimum of only two fully grown grain weevils in a pound of wheat (0.45 Kg) is sufficient to generate heating. Cooling it to at least 15°C is needed therefore to preserve the crop.

A more convenient method of storage in which maximum use is made of ventilation to reduce temperature and moisture content is achieved by storage in sacks rather than in bulk. The smaller unit of the sack enables water vapour and heat to dissipate more rapidly, provided that they are not stacked too close together so as to exclude the air. It has been calculated that a 100 Kg bag (2 cwt) open to the air will cool in 25 hours as much as a 3 metre square (10 ft sq) silo will cool in 8 weeks.[5]

The eggs of the insects can survive for long periods in cold, empty granaries without suffering any adverse effects, becoming active again when storage is renewed and the temperature is favourable.[6] Whilst inactive they tend to inhabit cracks in the granary fabric, in crevices and ledges in walls, or in holes in the flooring.[7] To minimise the dangers of infestation to the new crop of grain it is necessary to ensure that the walls are smooth and well plastered, and that the floor is free from cracks and holes which might provide harbourage for insects.

Considerable damage may also be caused by the entry of rodents to the granary, the most common pests being the rat (Rattus norvegicus Berk.), and the common mouse (Mus musculus L.). During the autumn and winter the granary provided ideal food and shelter for such creatures and much harm can be caused by gnawing and contamination. The main methods of combatting these pests before the advent of rat poison must have been primarily concerned with the prevention of entry by plugging holes in the fabric, providing some form of mesh over the ventilators, and blocking holes under the eaves. Birds also injure the grain and the best deterrent would have been to keep the building as dark as possible to dissuade them from flying in when the doors were opened.

The main requirements for the successful storage of grain both in the ancient and modern periods consist of the prevention of germination and insect infestation by maintaining a low temperature and moisture content, and the prevention of contamination and destruction by rodents and birds, by denying them any opportunity of access.

STRUCTURAL REQUIREMENTS FOR GRAIN STORAGE

Bulk grain exerts complex pressures upon its retaining walls and acts as a 'semi fluid'. It exerts lateral thrust against the walls of its enclosing bins and also against the external granary walls. A vertical pressure is applied to the floor by the sheer weight of the grain; for example, wheat exerts a pressure of 785 kg/m^3, and barley, 689 kg/m^3. In addition, another vertical force is added to the walls because of the friction created between the bulk of the grain and the surface of the wall. The relationship between these forces has been expressed by Janssen and simplified by Jamieson.[8]

The foundations must be substantial enough to withstand the vertical pres-sures imposed upon the floor. The strength and safety of the foundations are dependent upon the subsoil into which they are dug, and their depth. Rock, compact gravel and firm clean sand provide the safest foundations and will permit a safe maximum load of grain of from 27.3 tonnes/m^3 to 49.19 tonnes/m^3 upon firm sand to as much as 7.45-196.76 tonnes/m^3 upon hard rock.

In addition to the needs imposed by the actual pressure of the grain, the granary must incorporate certain other features. Low temperatures and moisture levels are maintained in a modern example by means of electric fans and air ducts; either above or below floor level. To prevent damp it is necessary to completely waterproof the granary; roofs, gables and eaves should be watertight and the pitch of the roof should be sufficiently steep to enable good drainage of rainwater, 22 degrees is recommended today. Surface water must not be allowed to accumulate in the vicinity, and adequate drainage around the perimeter should be provided to eliminate this.

It is also necessary to ensure that there is good access for loading and unloading purposes. There must be sufficient space in front of the loading area for vehicles to turn round and manoeuvre easily.

We must assume that the basic properties and problems of grain and other foodstuffs in storage have not changed substantially from the Roman period to the present day. Thus, many of the structural features which are today incorporated into granaries to minimise damage to the grain were in use during the Roman period and can be detected in the structural remains of stone built granaries which survive in Roman forts.

3. CLASSICAL REFERENCES TO GRAIN STORAGE

Some information concerning the conditions necessary for the storage of grain and other foodstuffs in the Roman period can be obtained from commentators on agricultural techniques of the Classical world.

In 160 B.C. Marcus Cato recommended that a mixture of chaff with the residue of crushed olives, amurca, should be smeared over the interior of the granary. Once this substance had dried he assured his readers that cooled grain could be stored inside quite successfully, without danger from mice or weevils.[9]

Varro, writing in 37 B.C. advocated that wheat should be stored in granaries above ground (sublimia), open to the draught on the east and north sides in order to prevent dampness. He also described examples in Hither Spain and Apulia where granaries were built above ground in such a way that the wind could cool them; both from the sides, by means of windows, and also from beneath. The walls and floor should be coated with either marble cement or clay mixed with chaff and amurca, both to prevent damage by insects and mice, and to make the grain firm. Other measures taken by farmers to prevent deterioration, according to Varro, included sprinkling amurca over the wheat, and using Chalcidian chalk or wormwood.[10]

However, if the grain has already become infested he suggests a cure. The grain should be taken outside in the sunshine and bowls of water should be placed around it in the hope that 'the weevils will congregate at these and drown themselves.'[11]

Vitruvius, in the early 20s B.C. agreed that granaries should have concrete floors and also a north or north-east aspect in order to ventilate the grain, for if it was not kept cool it would be damaged by weevils and rodents.[12]

In order to keep grain as dry as possible Columella (A.D. 60) advocated that grain and cereals should be stored in ventilated lofts, whilst oil and wine were kept below. He also described a method of storage in which the granary with a vaulted ceiling had its earthen floor first soaked with lees of oil then rammed down like opus signinum, and then overlain by a flooring of tiles and sand mixed with oil lees instead of water. The walls must be plastered with clay and oil lees mixed with dried leaves of the wild olive, and the joint between wall and floor must be well sealed to prevent insects from being harboured in the cracks. He warns against disturbing grain which is recognised to be infested for, rather than getting rid of the pests, they will only be distributed through the whole mass. However, if they are left undisturbed they will only be concentrated to a depth of a palm's breadth and the underlying crop will be undamaged.[13]

If long term grain storage is intended Columella suggests that the grain should be threshed twice to discourage weevils.[14]

In his Naturalis Historia (A.D. 77) Pliny summarises the main methods of grain storage and the controversies between different authorities on the subject. Some preferred brick granaries with walls a yard thick without any ventilators or windows. Others, like Vitruvius, preferred windows facing north or north-east. Some farmers did not use lime in the construction of their granaries because they believed that it damaged the corn. Some granaries were built of timber and supported in pillars to facilitate ventilation, but there were also those who believed that grain shrinks in bulk if the floor is raised. Pliny also recorded the practice of those who thought that they could best preserve the grain by hanging up a toad by one of its longer legs at the entrance of the granary prior to the entry of the corn.

Pliny himself was of the opinion that despite the various methods postulated, one of the main factors in the preservation of stored grain was storing it at the appropriate time. It was useless to store if the grain was insufficiently ripened, or when it was too hot, for both factors encouraged pests to breed. He advocated storing grain in the ear as the method by which it was least likely to suffer damage.[15]

Although the climatic conditions referred to by these Italian commentators differ from those prevailing in Britain the main principles concerning grain storage remain constant. The principal features which are emphasised by all these authors is the necessity to reduce the moisture content and temperature, and to minimise the activity of insect and rodent pests. It is possible to detect some of the methods of achieving these requirements in the study of granaries built by the Roman army in Britain.

4. A COMPARISON OF EXCAVATED STRUCTURES

Types

The predominant type of stone granary found in Roman forts in Britain is the single example, buttressed along its external walls. Other types which occur are variations on this basic type. Two single granaries may be paired, sharing a common central wall as at Hardknott and Benwell (Figs. 6, 11), or may be linked together either around a central courtyard as at Ambleside and Caerhun (Figs. 6, 7), or with a small space between the partition walls, such as at Housesteads and Templeborough (Figs. 11, 14). A third variation, in which two single granaries are placed end to end has only so far been discovered at Birrens (Fig. 6).

The choice as to whether to build single granaries or pair them together seems to have been governed by convenience on individual sites. Ease of access for loading and unloading may have been facilitated by the pairing of granaries, but this seems to have depended upon the choice of each fort builder a and does not seem to reflect their date of construction.

Sizes and Proportions

Sizes varied considerably from 48.46 x 13.41 m in the legionary granaries at Chester, to 14.12 x 5.28 m in the fortlet of Croy Hill. The majority ranged from 20 to 30 m in length and from 6 to 10 m in breadth. The double granaries were often almost square units, for example Hardknott and Templeborough, (Figs. 11, 14), although others such as Benwell and High Rochester (Figs. 6, 11) were more elongated. The width must have been governed to a large extent by the maximum practical roof span available without needing elaborate and inconvenient internal supports. The length seems, in most cases to have been dependent upon the distance available between the via principalis and via quintana. Despite the variations in dimensions the proportions (Appendix 4) appear quite constant and the ratio of length to breadth is approximately 3-4:1, although there are some notable variations, for example at Camelon, where the proportions are 5·3 or Gelligaer, 2:1.

Construction

One of the characteristic features of the Roman military stone-built granary is the substantial nature of its construction. Walls varied in thickness between 0.76 m and as much as 1.30 m. The actual construction of the walling differed: some examples consisted entirely of mortared ashlar blocks, such as Chester and Penydarren, whilst others were drystone built, as at Old Church, Brampton and Slack. Other examples consisted of a facing of ashlar with a mortared rubble core, visible at Drumburgh, Corbridge and Templeborough.

The majority had buttresses built along the long walls, and often also at the ends, usually an average of one metre square, and well bonded with the wall.

They were invariably regularly spaced. the distances between them varying from 1.50 m to 3 m. Where sufficient evidence survives it appears that they were paired across the width of the structure to support regularly spaced roof trusses. The dimensions of external walls and buttresses are tabulated below (Table 4, p.55).

A small number of granaries were unbuttressed; Bar Hill, Caernarfon, Corbridge Phase 1 (3 examples), Slack and Whitley Castle (Figs. 6,7,9,14). Current thinking on the Corbridge examples suggests that they were probably half-timbered above masonry sleeper walls; and they may have supported timber clad roofs rather than heavy tiles. The Bar Hill, Caernarfon and all three Corbridge unbuttressed granaries are Antonine; the dates of Slack and Whitley Castle are uncertain.

Foundations consisted predominantly of clay and cobble packed foundation trenches, either following closely the line of the walls and projecting buttresses, or extending to the outer face of the buttresses; e.g. Balmuildy and Newstead. The granaries at Chester had foundations of pebbles and sandstone in rock-cut trenches. Several examples were founded upon broad stone flagged rafts overlying rammed clay and cobbles; such as Ambleside, Benwell, Cramond, Gelligaer II, Haltonchesters,[66] and Old Church, Brampton.

Floor Supports and Flooring

The floors of the horrea could be supported in three different ways: either by means of transverse walls, longitudinal walls or pillars. Alternatively, the floor may not have been raised at all.

Transverse sleeper walls were usually built approximately 0.61 m wide and between 0.70 m and 0.90 m apart. They vary in number from six at Gelligaer II to seventeen at Castell Collen. Rickman has pointed out that the transverse sleeper wall was used first in the Trajanic stone granaries of the Welsh auxiliary forts of Gelligaer II, Castell Collen and Penydarren, (Figs, 8, 10, 13) and he believes that this method of construction reflects an early copying in stone of methods used in building timber granaries such as Fendoch or Inchtuthil.[16] Later examples occur at Great Chesters, which is possibly Hadrianic (Fig. 11), in the Antonine single granary at Lyne (Fig. 12), and into the late 170s A.D. in the east granary at Corbridge in its third structural phase (Fig. 9).

There are slight variations in the construction of transverse sleeper walls: some examples were continuous, such as at Castell Collen and Lyne (Figs. 8, 12), whilst others had a central break, probably to enable good circulation of air, as at Gelligaer II and Corbridge Phase 3. (Figs. 9. 10). Penydarren, on the other hand, seems to incorporate both features (Figs. 13).

Gelligaer and Penydarren also provide tolerably good evidence for the presence of timber flooring, and this combination of transverse sleeper wall supporting a timber floor seems to represent the earliest traces of stone-built military horrea in Britain, of the Trajanic-Hadrianic period.

Several of the granaries studied did not exhibit any form of raised floor at all, not because the remains had been ploughed or robbed, or missed by incompetent excavation, but because the floors were laid directly upon the ground and were not provided with elaborate ventilation systems. Brecon

Gaer and Caersws II had flagged floors laid upon the natural subsoil. Caernarfon and Templeborough had beaten clay floors, and Caerhun still retained 3-7 cm of decomposed cement, reminiscent of the granary floor described by Columella (see above, p.5). The use of stone flagging was sufficient to counteract rising damp and there was no need to raise it off the ground, as was necessary with timber floors. It is possible that these floors represent later modifications to the granaries in which all trace of raised floor supports had been removed. It is even possible that in some examples the floor was raised not by means of stone walls or piers, but by timber posts, such as those discovered in the German forts of Neiderbieber and Weissenburg, overlooked during excavation.[17] Professor G. D. B. Jones has located postholes 1.25 m apart running parallel both with the internal face of the external wall and with a longitudinal sleeper wall in the granary at Pumpsaint.[18] They have been interpreted either as part of a timber frame to tie the roof beams, or to support a timber floor. It is difficult to see why the stone sleeper walls should need to have been supplemented by timber posts which would have a relatively short life in comparison with their stone counterparts; we could be dealing here with an earlier series of timbers replaced subsequently in stone, or even the bases of scaffolding posts which must have been used in the granary's construction.

It is possible to give only very approximate dates to the examples of granaries without raised floors. Templeborough is thought to have been constructed in stone after A.D. 100,[19] Brecon Gaer after A.D. 140, Caersws II late Hadrianic-Antonine and Caerhun and Caernarfon to be possibly of Antonine date.[20]

By far the most common method of raising granary floors in Britain was the use of the longitudinal sleeper wall (plate IB). The walls may be continuous, as at Ambleside, Bar Hill, Chester, Lyne and Newstead (Figs. 6, 8, 12), or may have had breaks at regular intervals corresponding to the positions of the ventilators to provide an adequate circulation of air, such as Birrens, Corbridge Phase 4, Rough Castle and South Shields (Severan) (Figs. 6, 9, 14). Another variation is the use of only one continuous longitudinal sleeper wall, running down the centre of the building, exhibited at Old Church, Brampton (east) and Ribchester (north) (Fig. 13). It is not clear, however, just how valid this distinction is because there is the possibility that other parallel sleeper walls may have originally existed, but have been subsequently robbed or simply missed by the excavators. The number of parallel longitudinal sleeper walls varies from four at South Shields (Severan) to eight at Corbridge (east, Phase 4).

The date range for this method of floor support varies from the possible Hadrianic examples at Old Church, Brampton, the early second century at Chester, Antonine examples including Cadder, Camelon, Lyne, Newstead and Rough Castle, to the Severan examples at Corbridge Phase 4 and South Shields. Both timber and stone flooring seems to have been used; timber floors have been suggested for Ilkley and Ribchester (north). Others had flagged floors, such as Rough Castle (Antonine), and Birdoswald, Corbridge and South Shields in the Severan period. What little evidence we have suggests that the stone flagging of a raised floor may be more characteristic of Antonine or Severan construction than of an earlier period.

A fourth method of floor construction was used, in which stone pillars, arranged in parallel rows, supported the floor. (Plate IIIA). This method was used only infrequently; in fact only four examples are known in Britain, in marked contrast to the majority of German examples in which this method of floor support predominated.[21] Examples have been found at Castlecary, Housesteads, Ribchester (south), and South Shields (double granary). Housesteads, Ribchester and South Shields used squared stone pillars, whilst at Castlecary large boulders 30-45 cm in size were used. (Figs. 8, 11, 13, 14). The north granary at Housesteads revealed square sockets in the long walls to locate the cross members of a timber floor. Below them projected a ledge, upon which the floor joists would have rested. A similar ledge ran round the interior of the south granary at Ribchester, surviving to a height of 1 m. At Housesteads ventilators were provided in the long external walls which corresponded with gaps between the rows of pillars. (Plate IIIB). Pillars were also used in the Hadrianic double granary at Hardknott (fig. 11), but here only one central row was revealed in each half, consisting of seven piers.

Dating of these structures seems to be confined to the mid second century; Housesteads and South Shields are Hadrianic, Ribchester is undated, and Castlecary is of Antonine construction.

Examination and comparison of floor support methods does seem to suggest a sequence of construction techniques. The earliest examples, of Trajanic-Hadrianic date, utilised transverse sleeper walls; total absence of a raised floor is found predominantly in Hadrianic-Antonine contexts, as is the use of pillars. Although longitudinal sleeper walls were present in the Hadrianic period they seem to continue into the third century, and were used exclusively during the Severan period. Although some sort of sequence does seem to emerge it is very difficult to pinpoint it with any precision, or to really assess its validity.

The systems were not mutually exclusive. The Hadrianic granary at Haltonchesters contained north-south sleeper walls in the northern part, and east-west walls in the southern part, which appeared to be contemporary. Similarly the unbuttressed granary underlying Site XI at Corbridge had two longitudinal sleeper walls in the western half, and six transverse walls in the east (Antonine). The unfinished west granary of Phase 3 at Corbridge also contained two contemporary systems of sleeper walls. (Fig. 9). The single granary at Lyne had transverse walls whilst the large double granary h had longitudinal walling. Ribchester also exhibits these variations for one granary had longitudinal walls, and the other pillars.

So few structural details are often given in the excavation reports recording granaries that it is difficult to be sure whether the examples which were uncovered and planned are in fact contemporary, or whether the fort has yielded its full complement of granaries. It is necessary to know much more about the history of each individual structure and its relationship with other buildings in the fort. One may have been entirely refitted or demolished, or an extra one added at a particular period, and if successive rebuilding could be detected it might be possible to recognise changes, for example in the methods of floor support, or other significant features at specific dates. There is only one example which exhibits these characteristics, the pair of granaries from Corbridge which exhibit 4 structural phases. At Newstead it has been possible to detect a succession of building. Although both north and south granaries had similar cobbled foundations, the southern example was constructed with well dressed blocks of sandstone, showing no signs of modification, whilst the fabric of the north granary consisted of sandstone, blocks of blue greywacke from the riverbed, and pieces of reused tile and quern; factors indicating reconstruction. From this evidence the excavator, Mr. James Curle was able to deduce that although both granaries had stood simultaneously, at a later date, perhaps when the garrison was reduced the north granary was demolished but reconstructed later in the fort's history to coincide with the re-introduction of a larger garrison.[22]

Ventilators

Ventilators were pierced through the external walls in order, in conjunction with a raised floor, to achieve a good circulation of cool air. They were usually placed between each pair of buttresses on the long walls but there are variations, such as Castlecary (Fig. 8), where only the three central bays are pierced with ventilators. The openings varied in maximum width from 0.75 m at Chester to 0.30 m at South Shields. They either splayed inwards or were completely rectangular. Several examples display subsequent reductions in width by blocking; at Gelligaer the ventilators were reduced from 1 m to 0.60 m, and at Balmuildy from 0.45 m to 0.22 m.

Such large apertures would scarcely have excluded rodents and other small animals from entering the basement below the granary floor, and spillage of grain into this area, especially through cracks in a wooden floor would have provided a good harbourage for these pests. It must therefore have been necessary to cover the ventilation slits with a wooden or iron grill to prevent this. There seems to be little evidence for the survival of iron traces in these positions and it must be assumed that timber was used instead.

In his excavations at Cadder in 1929-31 John Clarke detected a 'black layer' 8 cm thick beside the walls in what appeared to be two distinct layers. He drew comparisons with other sites which had similar layers associated with the exterior of granaries. At Castlecary, a double layer of coal dross was detected, at Slack a layer of burnt material occurred which was not burnt again. Similarly there were strong signs of burning outside the second ventilator from the south angle on the south-west wall at Castell Collen. Clarke suggests that these layers represent periodical attempts to smoke out vermin.[23] In view of the problems which vermin must have caused by entering the ventilation channels it does seem feasible that occasionally when the granary was empty, the ventilators were perhaps blocked up and a fire lit at one end in order to smoke them out.

A couple of the granaries studied possessed an entrance in one of the short sides, not large enough for a proper doorway, but nevertheless provided with some form of doorframe, which was subsequently blocked. One occurs in the west granary at Corbridge (Phase 4), at Hardknott, and possibly also at Rough Castle (Fig. 11, 14). The excavator of the Corbridge example suggested that this may have been used to provide access during the building's construction and also later for periodic cleaning, or perhaps to keep rodents at bay.[24]

Loading platforms, porticos, entrances and drains

The short end wall of the granary was invariably used to provide access and there is no evidence for doorways being situated in the long walls. Several granaries possessed stone-built loading platforms constructed against one of these end walls, designed to facilitate the handling of large quantities of grain. In some instances they were incorporated with a portico to provide extra shelter during loading and unloading. Well preserved examples have been recorded at Corbridge, Hardknott, Ribchester, Rough Castle and Rudchester (Figs. 9, 11, 13, 14). They were of solid masonry construction and protruded between two and three metres. Other structures were less substantial, for example at Castlecary and South Shields (Severan), where one of the end walls was doubled in thickness in order to form a loading platform. Another method of construction is seen at Gelligaer II (Fig. 10) where the loading platforms were built across the full width of the granary, and situated at both ends. They consisted of an outer framework of well-dressed stones, infilled with rubble, and flagged. Examination of worn and unworn flagstones has led the excavator to suggest that a portico may have originally been constructed on their perimeter.[25] There are several examples where traces of foundations of loading platforms have been located although there is little evidence as to their nature, for example at Cadder, Cappuck, I Ilkley and Slack.

In the majority of granaries excavated no traces of loading platforms have been recorded. It is possible that in many instances timber platforms were used, leaving only the remains of postholes which may have been overlooked during excavation. On the other hand, it may sometimes have been necessary to utilise all the space allotted between the via principalis and via quintana for the construction of the granary, leaving insufficient extra space to allow a platform to protrude. On granaries without end buttresses it would have been quite possible to draw a cart alongside and unload its contents, without the aid of an intermediate platform. Where protruding end buttresses do occur this would have been impossible and it would have been necessary, in the absence of a loading platform, to perform the relatively difficult manoeuvre of backing the cart into the doorway.

The loading platform was only acting as an external projection of the internal floor, and it would have been no more difficult to lift sacks of grain directly from the cart to floor level than from the cart onto a loading platform. The main advantage is that the provision of a portico enables the bulk stores to be off-loaded in relatively sheltered conditions. It is possible to envisage the doors opening outwards to enclose the sides of the bay, providing a form of weatherproof tunnel through which the grain could be taken into the interior of the granary.

Porticos have been located at Benwell, Corbridge, Newstead, South Shields (Hadrianic) and Templeborough. At Benwell (Fig. 6), six rectangular piers remained, constructed upon splayed bases, in front of the building. At Corbridge (Phases 3 and 4) eight column bases remained. In both cases the width between the central piers was greater than between the lateral ones, thus giving more room for carts to manoeuvre to reach the central doors. Near the south-west corner of the south granary at Newstead (Fig. 12) was found a single column with a circular base, at a distance of 0.65 m from the west wall. It was believed by the excavator that this was the sole survivor of a portico originally situated on the west side of the granary.[26] The Hadrianic double granary at South Shields (Fig. 14) revealed the remains of three squared pillar bases. Perhaps the best surviving example is that of Templeborough (Fig. 14) where a portico was built along the south and east sides, consisting of four and seven columns respectively.

Although so few porticos have been located in association with granaries it is possible that many more may have originally existed. The columns may have been constructed of timber, and the verandah bonded to the granary above a level at which any evidence would survive archaeologically. Timber sockets may well have been overlooked in excavation. If the excavator was merely following the walls of the granary he is unlikely to have found a portico built at a distance of some metres from the external wall. This is also the case in the detection of associated drains. The example at Corbridge shows quite clearly an encircling drain (Fig. 9), but as they were built to drain water away from the eaves they are of necessity built at some distance from the granary wall, and thus if a large area in the vicinity of the granary was not examined such features may well have remained hidden. Several sites have revealed granary drains; either simple open gutters such as at Bar Hill and Birrens, or stone flagged, such as Corbridge and Templeborough. (Figs. 6, 9, 14).

Few of the examples showed any evidence of steps or entrances. The steps and threshold of the north granary at Housesteads still survive and there was also a flight of steps 2.89 m broad in the east granary at Benwell. Ribchester (south) and Slack also had steps remaining. The low incidence of survival of evidence for entrances may well be due to the fact that in many examples only the foundations survived subsequent stone robbing and cultivation, but the walls would have had to survive to the height of the floor level before such evidence could be expected.

Siting within the fort

The majority of granaries were located within the central range of principal buildings. Both single and double granaries were usually sited on one or both sides of the principia, with their short axis parallel with the via principalis. There are variations on this general picture. For example, although the single granaries at Gelligaer are situated in the central range on either side of the principia they are not immediately adjacent but are sited next to two of the gates. Some examples do occupy a central position but instead of flanking the principia two single granaries may be built next to each other, with their long axis parellel with the via principalis, for example, Birdoswald, Caernarvon and Castell Collen, and also the double at Templeborough. One of the main factors governing the siting of the granaries must have been concerned with convenience; the process of loading and unloading supplies must have been inconvenient to the running of the fort and their siting would have been chosen to minimise the obstruction caused.

Additional granaries were sited in various positions. The double granary at Birrens, (Fig. 6) for example, was situated on the opposite side of the via principalis to the single ones, with its long axis parallel. At Drumburgh a granary is sited in the north-west angle of the fort, at Chester-le-Street there is one placed next to the east gate, both examples presumably supplementing centrally positioned granaries.

In the legionary fortress at Chester three of the granaries have been located in the praetentura, next to the porta principalis dextra. Their situation outside the principal range seems to have been dictated by the necessity to be as near to the harbour gate as possible for greater east in unloading supplies.[27] Another variation in the general pattern is provided by the granaries at South Shields. In the Hadrianic period the double granary was situated in the prin-ciple range, next to the south-west gate, but during the Severan period the entire fort was converted into granary space (Fig. 3), in which twenty singles were constructed, each with their short axis parallel with the via principalis, and arranged in three parallel rows in the praetentura, principal range and half of the retentura.

The eccentric position of the recently excavated granary at Bearsden demonstrates that sometimes the siting was dictated by the topography of the site, in this case a steep north-south slope which had necessitated the construction of the granary along the slope.[28]

5. STRUCTURAL ASPECTS, AND THEIR INTERPRETATION

The surviving structural remains of these granaries illustrate many of the distinctive features which were designed by the Roman military engineers to overcome the problems of grain storage, outlined above.[29]

Maintenance of a low temperature was achieved by the air channels provided between the supports of the raised floor which, linked to ventilators in the external walls, produced a cool through draught of air. The combination of stone walling and stone flagging would have contributed significantly to this refrigeration effect, and would also have prevented rising damp from damaging the grain. However, even on a waterproof floor the bottom layer of grain tends to get damp because of the chilling, and it would have been advisable to store the grain on dunnage, wooden gratings of some kind, to prevent this.[30]

A suggestion has often been made in the past that the thick buttressed walls were necessitated by the great lateral thrust imposed by the loose grain stored within.[31] William Bulmer has pointed out, however, that the pressures exerted upon the external walls would have been no greater than those imposed upon the sides of internal timber bins. He postulates that the main strength of the building was provided by a series of strong masonry piers supporting the roof trusses in which the lengths of walling between, structurally weakened by the insertion of under floor ventilators and high level louvred openings, performed merely the function of weather proofing.[32]

In an attempt to test the validity of these conclusions calculations were made, taking the west granary at Corbridge as an example, in order to assess the structural strength of the walls and buttresses. Appendix 1 shows that the walls of the Corbridge example were quite adequate to withstand the pressures of grain stacked to a height in excess of 3 metres. Thus, although bulk grain does exert complex pressures on its retaining walls, it is clear that the width of the walls of the granaries studied were quite sufficient to counteract the lateral thrust of the grain.

The provision of external buttresses which are present in most of the granaries under consideration, do not seem to be linked primarily with resisting the pressures exerted by the grain. It is more probable that their function lies in supporting the heavy tiled roof and the complex of timber supports (Fig. 1). The Corbridge example shows quite clearly that the buttresses are paired across the width of the building and they probably bore the main horizontal roof timbers. The weight of a tiled roof of one of these buildings must have been considerable (Fig. 2). Quantities of tile debris have often been found during excavation, both _tegulae_ and _imbrices_. Tiles were present at several sites including Balmuildy, Chester and Gelligaer. Stone roofing slabs have been recovered from Ilkley and Haltonchesters, and slate from Ambleside.

The approximate weight of the roof at Corbridge has been estimated, based upon measurements and weights of several examples of <u>tegulae</u> and <u>imbrices</u> from the collection of the National Museum of Wales. (See Appendix 2.) The minimum weight of a tiled roof would be 28 tons, and, if the weight of timber (oak) trusses and supports is taken into consideration, it may be increased by at least a further 12 tons to make a minimum total of 40 tons.

Calculations to assess the smallest cross section of buttresses required to support such a roof weight have been included in Appendix 3. The results from two of the examples examined, Corbridge and Castlecary, show quite clearly that the buttresses alone would have been sufficiently strong to support the conjectured roof weights. Thus it is concluded that, although the problems of lateral thrust and weatherproofing must be taken into account, the prime function of the heavy buttressing was to uphold the heavy tiled roof. Other stone-built structures within the Roman fort must also have been tile-roofed, especially the <u>principia</u> and <u>praetorium,</u> but very few exhibit the characteristic buttressing of the granaries, with the exception of Birrens, Camelon, Cramond and Crawford II. It is possible that the basic courtyard plan of these buildings incorporating many more load bearing internal partitions and presenting smaller expanses to be roofed, presented fewer problems.

Tiled roofs would have made the granaries weatherproof, and in addition, an efficient method of drainage was essential to eliminate surface water and dampness in the vicinity of the granary. The roofs were also externally fireproof, a very important factor; destruction of the granary would render the garrison extremely vulnerable, especially those in outlying areas. It has been suggested that forts which were built entirely of timber, for example Inchtuthil, needed special precautions to eliminate the fire risk and thus the six granaries were not grouped together in the usual way but dispersed into opposite parts of the fortress to minimise the risks.[33]

The granary surviving to the greatest height which has so far been excavated is the one standing 2.75 m high in the Classis Britannica fort at Dover. Unfortunately it has been impossible to obtain any information concerning this structure except that "half way up the wall was a beam slot and various soffits", which has led the excavator to postulate a second storey.[34] Similarly, it has been suggested that the insertion of seven large pillars along the central axis of the east granary at Corbridge was done either to strengthen a sagging roof, or possibly to support a second floor.[35] The case for a second storey must be considered carefully. The thickness of the walls alone would easily be sufficient in many cases to confine the pressures of the grain, and the heavy buttressing tends to look disproportionate when a reconstruction is attempted, which may suggest the presence of a second floor. The need to store other foodstuffs such as vegetables, cheese, wine, meat and olive oil may have taken up extra space in a loft or second storey.[36] Several of the granaries studied have revealed external areas of cobbling against one of the long walls; features interpreted by their excavators as foundations for loading platforms. They have been observed at Caerhun, Mumrills and Old Kilpatrick. The position of these features against the long walls makes their interpretations as loading platforms unlikely. They may represent the foundations of stair-cases leading to an upper floor although one might imagine that, had staircases

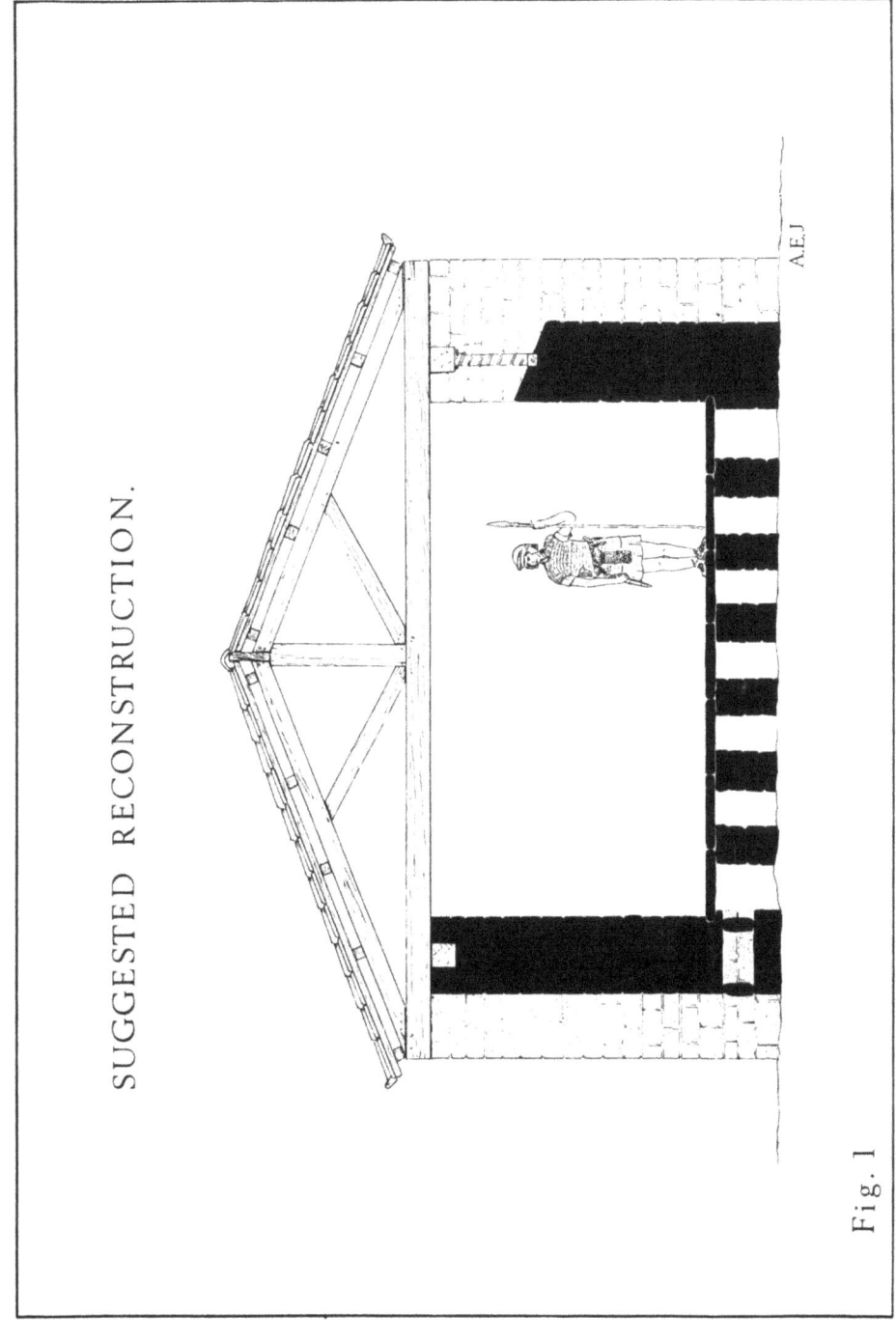

Fig. 1

existed, they would have been internal, for greater security. There may be some relevance in the fact that, disregarding orientation, many examples are situated to the north of the principia, a fact which might possibly suggest a two storeyed structure placed in a position where it was least likely to obscure the light to the principal administrative offices. In the absence of any conclusive evidence to the contrary, for the purposes of this study, it has been assumed that the military horrea were single storey structures.

There is no evidence at all to indicate the internal layout of the granary. In dealing with bulk grain three methods of storage are possible; either heaped directly onto the floor, confined in bins or stacked in bags or sacks. Previously all the calculations which have been made to assess the capacity of Roman granaries have assumed that the grain was stored in timber bins placed on either side of a central corridor. Haverfield and Collingwood envisaged bins 1.83 m (6 ft) deep with a corridor 0.90 m (3 ft) between them, covering the entire floor space available.[37] Professor Richmond, in his suggested reconstruction of the timber granaries at Fendoch postulated bins 1.50 m (5 ft) deep.[38] In his reappraisal of ration storage Mr. Bulmer believes that a 0.90 m wide corridor is insufficient, and that bins 1.50 m deep may have been used with a sloping base 30 cm off the ground at one end to enable the bin to empty completely. The loss in the amount of storage area by the use of the sloping base bin would amount to 30%, which he eliminates by raising the back of the bin to 1.98 m (6 ft 6 in). If this were done it would limit the amount of wall which could be pierced with louvred ventilators, for they would have to be built at a higher level than the top of the grain.

The walls of timber bins would have to withstand the same lateral thrust as the external walls and therefore they must have been keyed into the floors and walls in some way to prevent them from slipping forward under the weight of the grain. Although it is true that the timber floors which may have provided this evidence have long since perished, had timber bins been constructed upon stone flagged floors, such as at Corbridge, one would expect to find the sockets or timber slots into which the bins had located; features which have not yet been recorded.

It is feasible that bulk grain could have been stored loose on the floor. This method would have been extremely inconvenient. It would have been difficult to separate fresh grain from old stock, and rotation would have been impeded. Handling would also have been hampered because the loose grain would behave as a liquid and be very difficult to contain successfully.

The most practical and convenient method of storing and handling would seem to be the use of containers, either sacks or wicker baskets, although the sack would be preferable. The whole idea of the provision of a loading platform suggests that the grain was entering the granary in some form of container and was not being shovelled loose from the cart onto the loading platform and then into the interior. This method would also make the rotation of stock easier. In the case of store depots, such as South Shields, which must have had a frequent turnover of stock, it is difficult to imagine any other system of storage being practicable.

Bulmer dismisses the idea of ladling corn from the top of the bin to each individual soldier queuing up for his grain ration because of the inefficiency

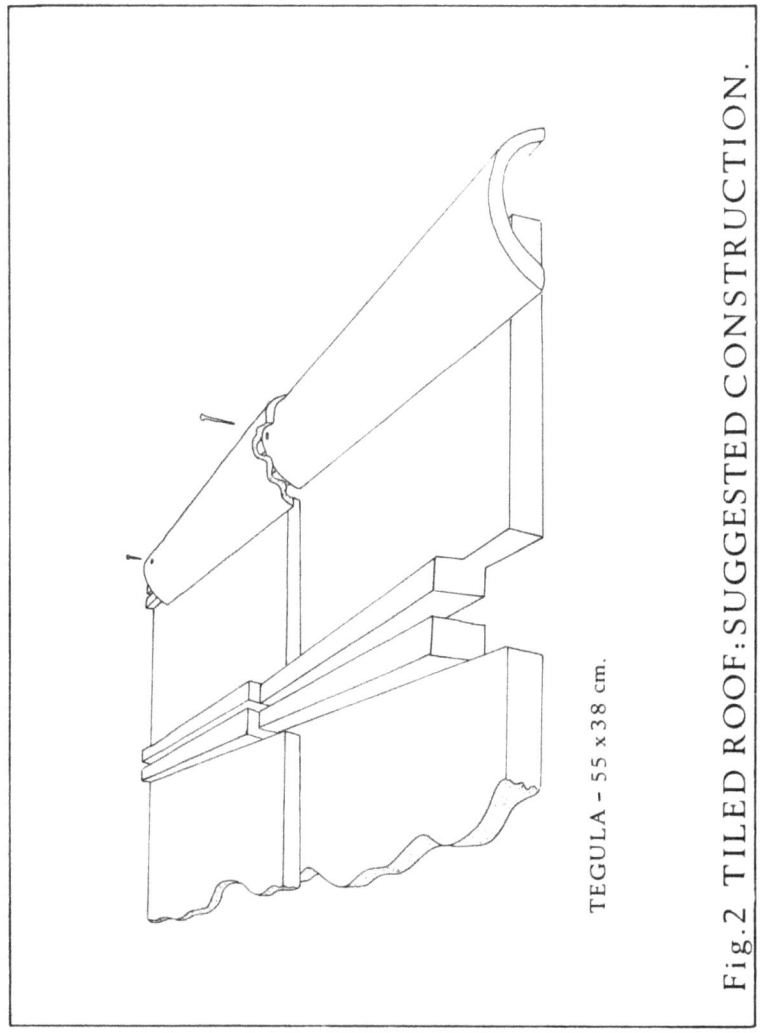

TEGULA - 55 x 38 cm.

Fig. 2 TILED ROOF: SUGGESTED CONSTRUCTION.

and chaos which this would cause. As an alternative he suggests the use of a bin with discharge chute and shutter.[39] But the notion of 500 or 1000 men queueing up daily to receive their grain ration seems unrealistic and time consuming. Surely it would have been more convenient for a measured quantity appropriate perhaps to a century, or smaller unit to be collected by one or two men either daily or weekly, to be distributed amongst the remainder upon their return to the barrack area.

The standard modern sack weighs 63.5 kg, and is the convenient lifting and handling size for one man. If we assume that each man was supplied with 1 kg of grain per day (see below, page 25), a century consisting of between 80 and 100 men would require 80-100 kg. Two sacks would easily suffice for the daily needs of a whole century, and this method of distribution seems more probable.

Within permanent forts each century appears to have been responsible for grinding its own grain, and possessed its own mill and baking ovens.[40] Millstones bearing centurial inscriptions have been recovered from Weisbaden bearing the words: C(enturia) C(ai) Rufi; and two such stones from Mainz bear the inscriptions C(enturia) Virei and C(enturia) Vet.[41]

Examination of similar stones from the Saalburg has led Jacobi to reconstruct the mill from which they were derived as a 'slave' mill in which a large handle on a horizontal axis was turned to drive geared stones on a vertical axis at a higher speed, corresponding in its major elements to the classic Vitruvian water mill. He calculated that between four and six men could grind 100 kg of grain, the amount needed daily by a century, in one hour.[42] Moritz, on the other hand, suggests an alternative reconstruction in which an animal can drive a vertical shaft connected at a higher level to the geared mill.

In addition, several much smaller stones have been noted by Jacobi, both from the Saalburg and from several other sites, including Newstead. One such example from the Saalburg bears the inscription: Con(tubernium) Brittonis. It is clear therefore that such stones were issued to the contubernium consisting of 8-10 men. The use of these portable hand querns may have been confined to the army on the march rather than in permanent garrison, although there seems no reason why smaller groups should not have ground additional supplies.

The provision of bakehouses and ovens in Roman forts in Britain is, as yet, poorly known. However, evidence from the extensively excavated Agricolan fort at Fendoch may shed some light upon cooking arrangements. Five ovens consisting of platforms of flat stones each covered by a dome of rough stones infilled with clay were located in the back of the rampart opposite the end of each barrack block, suggesting that each oven served one century. The excavator supposed that each contubernium took its turn on a rota to cook the daily rations.[43]

Excavations of other forts such as Pen Llystyn and Birrens suggest also the presence of large well built 'official' ovens probably serving a centurial unit, with further more haphazard small ovens situated at the base of the rampart nearer the barrack quarters perhaps to cater for individuals or small groups.[44]

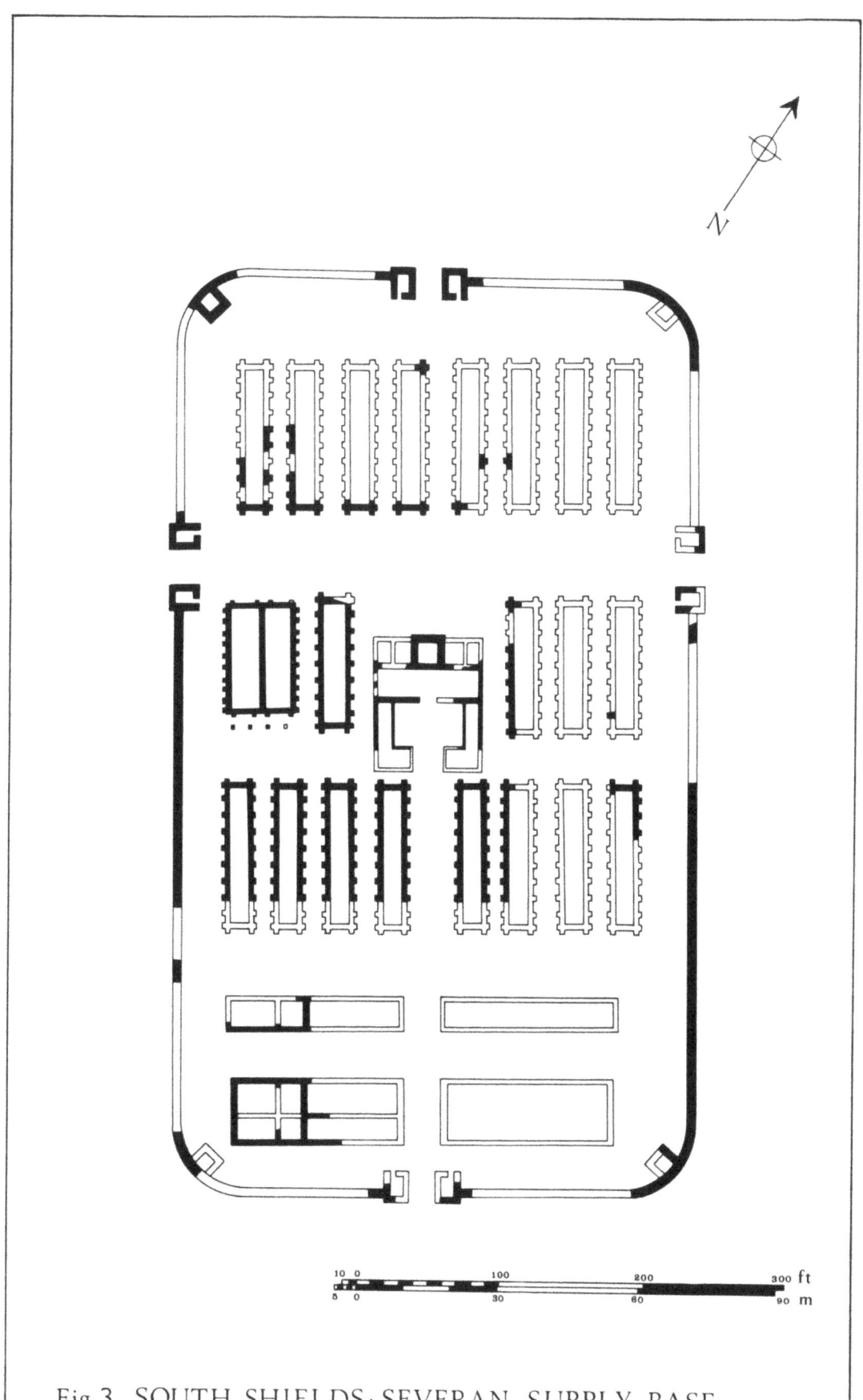

Fig.3 SOUTH SHIELDS: SEVERAN SUPPLY BASE.

Thus it seems probable that the sacks of grain appropriate perhaps to each century for a day's ration was collected from the granary, ground upon the century's own mill, baked, and only then distributed to the individual soldiers.

6. PROVISIONING OF ROMAN FORTS AND THE CAPACITY OF GRANARIES

It has been estimated by modern writers that the normal ration of grain consumed by one man in a day was 3 lb (1.36 kg). Taking this figure, calculations have been made to assess the possible requirements of a garrison and the amount of storage space necessary to house them.[45] Two independent assessments have been made of this figure, the first based upon research into Classical weights and measures, and the second by practical experiment.

There is a little contemporary evidence for rations and supplies in the Roman army. Polybius, writing c. 140 B.C. describes the pay of different ranks of soldiers and also their monthly corn allowance:[46]

Legionary: infantry soldier received 2/3 Attic medimnus = 28.3 kg
cavalry soldier receives 7 medimni barley = 258.0 kg
2 medimni wheat = 84.8 kg

Auxiliary: infantry soldier receives 2/3 Attic medimnus = 28.3 kg
cavalry soldier receives 1 + 1/3 medimni wheat = 56.5 kg
5 medimni barley = 184.3 kg

The allowance per day equals:

Legionary: infantryman = 0.94 kg (1.88 lb)
cavalryman = 8.60 kg (18.92 lbs) of barley
= 2.83 kg (6.23 lbs) of wheat

Auxiliary: infantryman = 0.94 kg (1.88 lb)
cavalryman = 1.88 kg (3.76 lbs) of wheat
= 6.14 kg (13.50 lbs) of barley

The Attic medimnus was equivalent to 6 Roman modii or 2 amphorae.[47] In modern terms it is equal to nearly 12 gallons.[48] The modius was approximately 2 gallons (15.36 pints). Dry measures of such commodities as grain were reckoned in pints and gallons. The normal dry measure weight and metric capacity were worked out by obtaining 1.36 kg (3 lbs) measures of wheat and barley.

One pint of wheat was found to weigh 0.46 kg, and a gallon, 3.68 kg. A medimnus would contain 42.39 kg and a modius 7.07 kg. One pint of barley weighed 0.40 kg, giving the weights of a medimnus and modius as 36.86 kg and 6.14 kg respectively. It is upon these figures that the above statement of Polybius has been interpreted.

Another reference to the grain requirements of the Roman soldier occurs on ostraca from Pselcis (modern Dakkeh). These records include receipts for food and wine for a cohors equitata, probably II Ituraeorum.[49] Several receipts ranging in date from Nov. 179? to Sept. 205 (A.D.) refer to the grain ration of a soldier per month as one artaba.

The artaba was originally a Persian dry measure equalling, according to Herodotus, 1 Attic medimnus and 3 choenices = 12.75 gallons approx. However, it was also an Egyptian measure consisting of an old measure, = 4.5 Roman modii = approx. 9 gallons; or a new artaba which equalled 3 and one third modii, or 6.5 gallons.[50] The new artaba was more common and it has been presumed that by the end of the 2nd century A.D. this was the measure to which the receipts refer.

If one Roman modius contained 15.36 pints, 3.33 modii = 51.2 pints, and an artab would weigh 23.6 kg (the monthly individual ration). The daily ration would be 0.80 kg (1.75 lb).

The modius from Carvoran was found to contain almost 20 pints, which would measure a quantity of approximately 9 kg of wheat.[51] Taking the average daily ration suggested above this modius could supply the needs of ten men. The smallest unit accommodated within the military barracks was a contubernium of, theoretically, ten men. However, it is to stray too far into the realms of supposition to link these two factors, and it is more likely that this modius represented some form of standard imperial measure which would not have been in daily use for measuring out rations.

The references which are available do seem to indicate that the daily grain ration for the infantry soldier was lower than 1.36 kg and was probably nearer 1 kg (2.21 lbs).

In order to examine the actual quantity involved a 1.36 kg sample was obtained. Clearly it is impossible to answer even fundamental questions involving the appetite of the Roman soldier, but nevertheless a 1.36 kg uncooked weight of cereal does appear to be more than adequate. The sample was milled in a rotary grinder and mixed with water to test the binding property of the flour, but the quantity of bran inhibited the production of a proper dough, and when baked a crude 'cake' resulted. There was no loss in weight between the original sample and the end product. The quality of Roman military flour cannot be known with any certainty, but Pliny in his <u>Natural History</u> states that: "It is a sure law of nature that with all kinds (of wheat) army bread is heavier by one third than the grain." Moritz points out that this kind of bread yield, when compared with modern equivalents, would most probably have been derived only from wholemeal or from meal of approximately 95% extraction.[52] This experiment demonstrated that a considerable amount of preparation was necessary to produce flour suitable for bread making. It would seem unlikely that a large group of men would either want to, or be allowed to, spend the amount of time necessary to produce flour for baking daily. For, one man producing a loaf with an individual quern would take the same time as a large communal mill producing bread flour for a larger number.

From these considerations two main points emerge. Firstly, the notion that perhaps the Classical reference to a 'daily or monthly' ration is a token reference to the amount of grain which should theoretically be allocated per head within the garrison; whether each man actually received his complete grain ration directly from the granary cannot be determined on the present evidence. Certain epigraphic information does exist which may help to clarify this point a little. Several of the ostraca from Pselcis record receipts by individuals for individual monthly grain rations, another example illustrates a receipt for 50 artabas which is signed by the fifty men concerned.[53] But it is not absolutely clear whether these are references to individual allocation and responsibility or whether it is part of formal Roman military procedure for men to have to sign receipts periodically, perhaps monthly, for materials received.

The second consideration is that the preparation of bread flour is a lengthy and relatively specialised process, whilst the preparation of a simple cereal food such as porridge is quicker and involves much less effort. It is possible that part of the ration was allocated to the men from the granary for this purpose whilst the rest would be alloted to the bakery, cooking bread for larger units. This would eliminate the need for large numbers of individual querns and ovens.

Taking the estimate of 1 kg of grain as each man's daily consumption it is possible to calculate, very approximately, the possible requirements of a garrison, and to see what relationship this bears to the storage area available within the granary. One man would require 365 kg annually, and a garrison of 500 men, 182,500 kg annually. Calculations may also be attempted to estimate the amount of storage space needed for such quantities. The weights and volumes of various cereals have been tabulated below:[54]

Commodity	kg/m^3	$m^3/tonne$
Wheat	785	1.3
Barley	705	1.4
Oats	513	1.9
Rye	705	1.4
Maize	753	1.3

Thus 785 kg of wheat occupy 1 cubic metre of storage space. The space needed to house the grain ration of 500 men would be: $182\,500/785 = 232.5$ cubic metres, if the grain was stored in bulk. If the grain was stored in sacks, the volume required would be increased by 15%, to give the total storage required for the rations of 500 men as 267.4 cubic metres.[55]

Theoretically it should be reasonably straightforward to compare these figures with the floor areas provided by horrea in Roman forts and to estimate the size of the grain supply in storage and the length of time for which it could supply a garrison of a certain size. Taking as the basis for their study the statement of Tacitus that Agricola secured his forts from protracted seige with supplies sufficient to last a year, annuis copiis, Haverfield and Collingwood attempted to estimate the capacity of each of thirteen granaries by assuming that the grain was stored to a height of 1.83 m, in bins 1.83-2.44 m wide, with a 0.90 m corridor. Their calculations assured them that the examples studied were able to store twice the quantity of grain required in a year.[56]

Similar calculations may be attempted for three examples:

1. Gelligaer - two granaries, each 16.15 x 7.01 m internally. If a 1.50 m corridor is left down the centre of each granary, the storage space in each would be $2.75 \times 16.15 \times 2\ m^2$. If the grain was stacked 2.5 m high in one

granary the space occupied would be 222 m^3, requiring the other 45 m^3 to be accommodated in the other granary in order to feed the supposed garrison, a cohors quingenaria peditata, for a year.

2. Housesteads - two sides of a double granary both 23.78 x 5.49 m internally. Allowing a 1.50 m corridor, storage space on one side would be 2 x 2 x 23.78 m^2. If the grain was stacked 2.5 m high in one granary it would provide storage space for 237.8 m^3. The garrison of the fort is thought to have been a cohors milliaria peditata, and both granaries would have had to have been stacked with sacks to a height of 2.8 m to supply such a garrison for a year.

3. Caerhun - two sides of a double granary, both 20.57 x 6.86 m internally. Allowing a 1.50 m corridor, the storage area on one side would be 2 x 2.68 x 20.57 m^2. If the grain was stacked 2.5 m high in one side it would provide storage for 275.6 m^3, sufficient to supply the supposed garrison, a cohors quingenaria equitata for a year, leaving the other side empty. It must be remembered, however, that no provision for horse fodder has been made.

However, there are too many unknown factors to make this kind of calculation really meaningful. Unless the fort has been totally excavated it is not possible to know whether the full complement of granaries has been discovered. There may have been granaries additional to those in the central range situated in other parts of the fort, as illustrated at Drumburgh (Fig. 10), Chester-le-Street, or Birrens. Without knowing exactly how many men the granaries had to supply or the number of animals to be maintained, and in the absence of accurate knowledge as to the daily grain allocation it is impossible to make finite statements concerning grain reserves and capacities. It is not possible to know the quantities of other foodstuffs stored, nor of the proportion of the Roman military diet which the grain ration represented.

The main emphasis is thought to have been on the storage of cereals, but many other foods must have been stored in the granary; the low temperature and adequate ventilation would have served as a large-scale refrigerator to preserve a large variety of foodstuffs, and the solidity of the construction would have provided greater security for the entire garrison's provisions. These must have included bacon, cheese, lard, olive oil, vegetables, sour wine and meat.[57] There may even have been some provision for the hanging of carcasses from the rafters in much the same manner as a modern cold store. Several Classical authors, and a painting from Pompeii, describe the use of the carnarium, a frame suspended from the ceiling comprising a series of hooks upon which provisions were hung, used in the kitchen and the tavern. It is equally possible that such devices may have been used in military horrea.[58] Despite the lack of contemporary references the large number of animal bones from Roman military sites reveal that a great deal of meat was eaten.[59] Vegetable remains have been recorded at Caer Sws and cabbage identified from Chesterholm; an ostraca from Pselcis also records a receipt for lentils, salt and vinegar. Wine would probably have also been stored within the granary, and several have revealed amphora fragments during excavation, such as Balmuildy and Ilkley.

The main emphasis was on cereals, however, and many examples of charred wheat have been found in granaries during excavations; a large quantity of charred wheat was discovered at Ribchester and smaller quantities from Ambleside, Birrens, Castell Collen, Great Chesters, Haltonchesters and Ilkley, whilst carbonised wheat and barley came from Brough by Bainbridge. The quantities recovered have been too small to give an overall picture of the cereals preferred by the army, but from his examination of carbonised grain from a late 1st-early 2nd century hut at Caerleon, Dr. Helbaek has been able to identify spelt, barley and possibly rye.[60]

There are several other factors which must be taken into consideration. Despite the statement of Tacitus (see page 25), it is not known for how long the supplies were supposed to last; there may have been instances where it was absolutely necessary for a fort to have a year's supply in reserve, whereas in others it is quite feasible that only a few months' or weeks' supply may have been needed, dependent upon the relative security and strategic position of the fort. It is clear that South Shields was a supply depot for Severan activities further north, but there may well have been other forts which also held reserve supplies to pass on to frontier posts as the need arose, so that a system may have acted as a chain of supply, perhaps with reserves at strategic points (Fig. 4). It may have become necessary to reinforce certain areas thus placing increased demand on the supplies of the locality. In this sort of situation it seems impractical to imagine the unit needing to wait for and depend upon supplies from a distant depot. It seems more feasible that a reciprocal operation would be in force, whereby reserve stores of grain could be passed on from holding depots, which themselves could be replenished subsequently more readily from a main supply base.

Perhaps a more valid way of assessing granary capacities in relation to possible garrison and fort size, in the absence of any epigraphic aid, is to equate the amount of space devoted in the fort to granaries, relative to the total fort area. Even then it is not possible to say exactly what function the fort performed, or how many men were in permanent garrison. It must be necessary to fall back on the assumption that if a large enough cross section is examined some kind of proportional pattern may emerge, and anomalies may become apparent. Comparison has been made between the amount of granary floor storage space available and the internal area of the fort which it served. In Table 1 the basic information is provided, and the internal and external fort area (in hectares and square metres), and the granary floor area available are expressed proportionally. In Fig. 5 the proportional patterns which emerged have been compared. In instances where there is some evidence to suggest the presence of a second granary, although it has not been fully excavated, the floor area has been assumed to equal that of the extant example, and the possible additional area has been stippled. A second granary has only been suggested where there is some firm evidence from the excavator for its existence as at Castlecary, or at Birdoswald, where two granaries have been detected by aerial photography.[61]

It can be seen that there is, broadly speaking, a relatively constant relationship between fort size and the area devoted to granaries, whether in the legionary base at Chester or the fort at Housesteads. It is reasonable to assume that this is a relationship in terms of the number of men accommodated in the fort, leaving aside the problems caused by the additional requirements of cavalry detachments. Several anomalies appear, notably Benwell, Birrens,

Haltwhistle Burn, Lyne and South Shields (Severan). The latter appears to have been a base used to supply the Severan Scottish campaigns. It has been suggested that Benwell held additional supplies in reserve for other forts along the Wall line as it was the furthest point up the Tyne which was navigable.[62] Haltwhistle Burn fortlet seems to have a granary far in excess of the needs of the small garrison which could have been catered for, and may have functioned as a reserve. It is possible that Drumburgh, with one granary built so close to the north-west angle, may have possessed more, and may have held reserve provisions to supply forts along the Wall from the west, replenished by sea from further south. Perhaps when further excavation has been carried out a clearer picture of the supply and distribution of the grain and supplies may emerge.

Table 2 sets out the theoretical annual grain requirement, in cubic metres, of the forts listed in the catalogue based upon their presumed garrisons. For these purposes, it has been assumed that the grain is stored to a height of 2 m (see page 25). An additional table has been added (Table 3) to show the relationship with six of the more fully excavated timber examples. Although the tables are based essentially upon conjecture some interesting results can be seen. For example, the fully excavated fort of Housesteads has revealed ten barrack blocks, each with 10-11 contubernia, implying a garrison of a cohors milliaria peditata. Its theoretical annual grain requirement, based on previous calculations (see page 25), would be 535 m^3; the capacity of the granary if stacked to a height of 2 metres would be 522 m^3. This need not, of course, imply that the formula can be extended to other forts and indeed it can be seen that many would, using this formula, possess granary storage capacities roughly twice the theoretical annual requirement necessary for their presumed garrisons. However, in many cases it must be remembered that the garrisons have only been suggested from interpretation based upon partial excavation of the fort's interior.

The most apparent discrepancy is associated with granaries in forts which are presumed to have housed cohors quingenaria, either peditata or equitata, e.g. Ambleside, Balmuildy, Haltonchesters etc., which appear to have a granary capacity of roughly twice their theoretical annual requirement. On the other hand those forts thought to house cohors milliaria, broadly speaking, correspond. These inconsistencies may be seen as a reflection of our lack of knowledge of the internal layout of the fort, difficulties in the identification of stabling, the assumption of a smaller garrison than was actually present, the holding of grain supplies in excess of Tacitus' annuis copiis, or finally, that certain forts held grain reserves to pass on to other garrisons. The issue is complex, but from these results it is clear that the study of military granaries does have an important contribution to make in any consideration of the garrisoning of Roman forts.

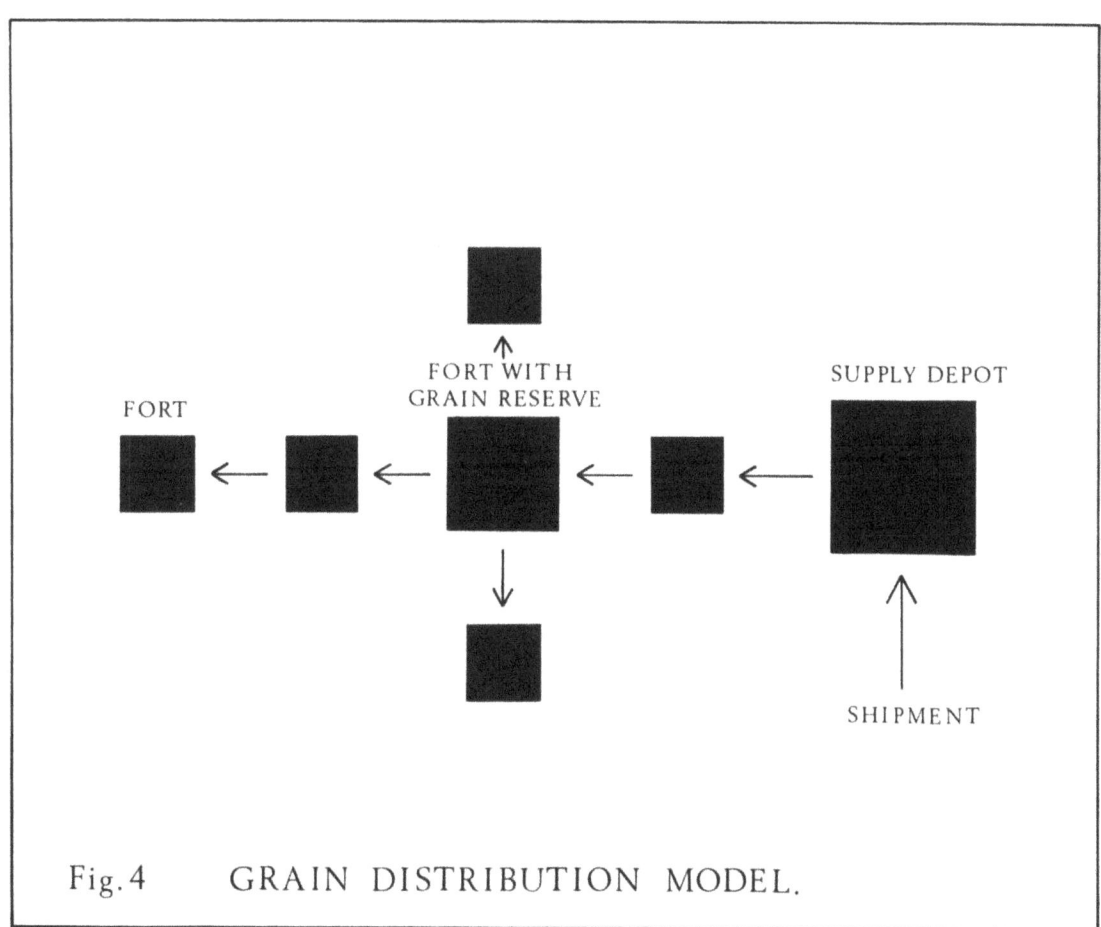

Fig. 4   GRAIN DISTRIBUTION MODEL.

TABLE 1

GRANARY FLOOR AREA EXPRESSED AS A PROPORTION OF THE
TOTAL INTERNAL FORT AREA

Fort	Area (ha) Overall	Internal	sq m	Granary floor area (sq m)	Proportion
Ambleside	1.22	1.04	10,400	228.6	2.2
Balmuildy	1.76	1.32	13,200	271.7	2.1
Bar Hill	1.37	1.29	12,900	210.5	1.6
Benwell	?2.24	?1.84	? 18,400	?613.7	?3.3
Birrens	1.97	1.65	16,500	475.8	2.9
Brecon Gaer	3.14	2.57	25,700	270.0	1.1
Cadder	1.34	1.15	11,500	159.3	1.4
Caerhun	1.97	1.60	16,000	282.2	1.8
Caernarfon	2.27	1.97	19,700	317.6	1.6
Caersws II	3.11	2.50	25,000	170.9	0.7
Camelon	3.69	2.41	24,100	130.2(240.8)	0.5(1.5)
Cappuck	0.60	0.50	5,000	46.9	0.9
Castell Collen	1.77	1.46	14,600	179.5	1.2
Castlecary	1.58	1.48	14,800	115.6(115.6)	0.8(1.6)
Castledykes	3.69	2.46	24,600	303.9	1.2
Chester	24.33	23.42	234,200	1591.3 (1591.3)	0.7(1.4)
Chesters	2.35	1.96	19,600	172.0	0.9
Crawford II	0.79	0.61	6,100	95.5	1.6
Croy Hill	0.80	0.62	6,200	45.8	0.7
Gelligaer II	1.49	1.15	11,500	226.4	2.0
Haltonchesters	1.75	1.48	14,800	?330.0	2.2
Haltwhistle	0.32	0.28	2,800	85.2	3.0
Hardknott	1.31	1.07	10.700	135.4	1.3
High Rochester	2.01	1.70	17,000	359.2	2.1
Housesteads	2.10	1.73	17,300	261.1	1.5
Ilkley	0.97	0.70	7,000	152.8	2.2
Lyne	2.61	2.24	22,400	861,0	3.8
Mumrills	2.86	2.64	26,400	236.8	0.9
Newstead	6.20	5.40	54,000	753.8	1.4
Old Church	1.52	1.27	12,700	273.3	2.2
Old Kilpatrick	1.91	1.68	16,800	132.2(158.0)	0.8(1.7)
Ribchester	2.50	2.00	20,000	314.2	1.6
Rough Castle	0.66	0.42	4,200	97.1	2.3
Rudchester	1.85	1.51	15,100	246.8	1.6
Slack	1.50	?1.30	? 13,000	191.7	1.5
South Shields (Had.)	2.09	1.73	17,300	261.4	1.5
(Sev.)	"	"	"	2506.5	14.5
Stanwix	3.77	3.65	36,500	254.4(254.4)	0.7(1.4)
Templeborough	?1.83	1.37	13,700	318.9	2.3

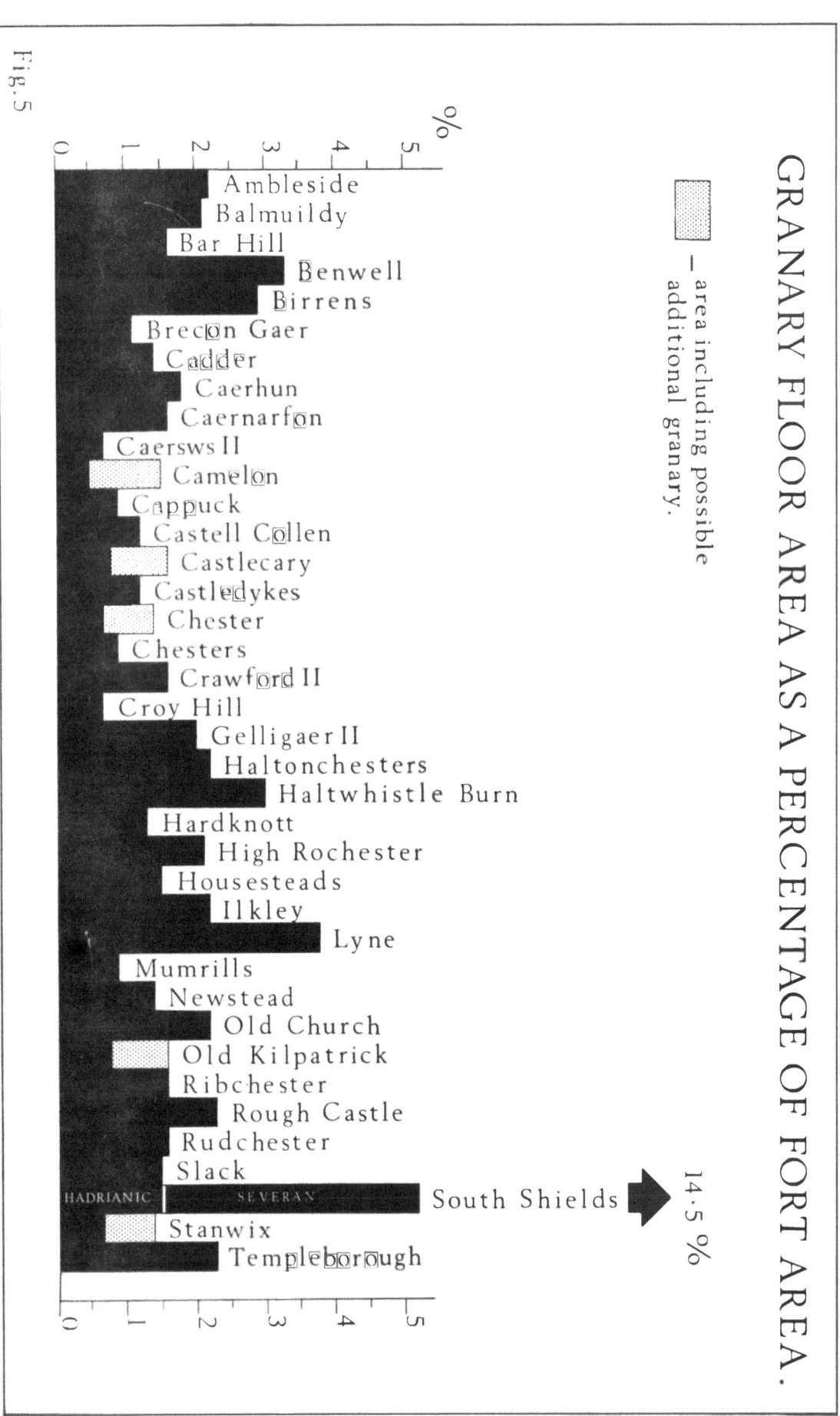

Fig. 5 GRANARY FLOOR AREA AS A PERCENTAGE OF FORT AREA.

TABLE 2

Fort	Granary floor area (m²)	Presumed garrison	Capacity if grain stored to height of 2 m (m³)	Theoretical annual requirement (m³)
Ambleside	228.6	coh. quingenaria	457.2	267.4
Balmuildy	271.7	coh. quing. eq.	543.4	267.4
Bar Hill	210.5	coh. quing.ped.	421.0	267.4
Benwell	613.7	ala quingenaria	1227.4	267.4
Birrens	475.8	coh. mill.eq.	951.6	534.8
Brecon Gaer	270.0	ala quingenaria	540.0	267.4
Cadder	159.3	coh. quingenaria	318.6	267.4
Caerhun	282.2	coh.mill.eq.	564.4	534.8
Caernarfon	317.6	coh. milliaria	635.2	534.8
Caersws II	170.9	ala quingenaria	341.8	267.4
Camelon	130.2(371.0)	?	260.3(742.0)	?
Cappuck	46.9	less than cohort	93.7	?
Castell Collen	179.5	coh.quingenaria eq.	358.9	2.4
Castlecary	115.6(115.6)	coh.mill.eq.	231.2(x 2)	534.8
Castledykes	303.9	?	607.8	?
Chester	1591.3(1591.3)	legion	3182.6(x 2)	3208.8
Crawford II	95.5	less than cohort	190.9	?
Croy Hill	45.8	less than cohort	91.5	?
Gelligaer II	226.4	coh.quing.eq.	452.8	267.4
Halton	330.0	coh.quing.eq.	660.0	267.4
Haltwhistle	85.2	less than cohort	170.3	?
Hardknott	135.4	coh. quingenaria	270.8	267.4
High Rochester	359.2	coh. quingenaria	718.4	267.4
Housesteads	261.1	coh.mill.ped.	522.2	534.8
Ilkley	152.8	coh. quingenaria	305.5	267.4

Lyne	861.0	?	1722.0	?
Mumrills	236.8	ala quingenaria	473.6	267.4
Newstead	753.8	leg.vex + ala quing. ?	1507.7	?
Old Church	273.3	?	546.6	?
Old Kilpatrick	132.2(158.0)	coh. milliaria	264.4(580.4)	534.8
Ribchester	314.2	?	628.4	?
Rough Castle	87.1	less than cohort	194.2	?
Rudchester	246.8	coh.quing.eq.	493.5	267.4
Slack	191.7	?	383.3	?
South Shields (H)	261.4	ala quingenaria	522.7	267.4
Stanwix	254.4(254.4)	ala milliaria	508.9(x 2)	534.8
Templeborough	318.9	coh. milliaria	637.8	534.8

33

TABLE 3

TIMBER GRANARIES

	Internal area (ha)	Granary floor area (m^2)	Proportion	Possible garrison	Capacity if grain stored to ht. of 2 (m^3)	Theoretical annual requirement (m^3)
Baginton II	1.4	390	2.8	coh. quing.	780	267
Crawford I	0.6	84	1.4	4 turmae	167	70
Fendoch	1.4	312	2.2	coh.mill.ped.	624	535
Hod Hill	2.8	108	0.4	leg.vex+half coh. quing.	217	172
Inchtuthil	20.4	3183	1.6	legion	6367	3209
Pen Llystyn	1.6	442	2.9	2 quing. cohs.	884	535

APPENDIX 1

CALCULATION TO ASSESS THE CAPABILITY OF THE WALLS OF THE CORBRIDGE WEST GRANARY (PHASE 4) TO WITHSTAND THE LATERAL THRUST EXERTED BY THE GRAIN IN STORAGE

Let wall thickness = t
Let height of grain stacked against wall = h
Let lateral thrust of level grain = T
Let the mass of the wall = M

$M = \rho gV$ Where ρ is the density of the wall material, V is the volume and g is the acceleration due to gravity.

$M = \rho$ whtg per metre width.

Assuming that the grain is stored in a bin whose length and breadth are equal to the height,

$$T = \rho g \times \frac{h^2}{2} \times \frac{h}{3} g$$

- the maximum pressure is assumed to be at one third of the way up the wall. For equilibrium, and taking moments about 0:

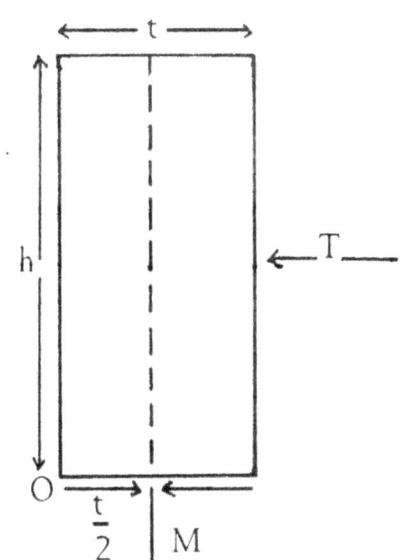

$$\rho wght \times \frac{t}{2} = \rho g \frac{h^2}{2} \times \frac{h}{3} g$$

$$\rho w t^2 = \rho g \frac{h^2}{3}$$

$$t = \sqrt{\frac{\rho gh}{3\rho w}}$$

Assuming

$\rho w = 2200$ kg/m^3 63

$\rho g = 785$ kg/m^3 64

Taking the height, h as 3 m,

$$t = \sqrt{\frac{785 \times 3}{3 \times 2200}} \text{ m} = 0.60 \text{ m}$$

Taking the height as 2.5 m,

$$t = \sqrt{\frac{785 \times 2.5}{3 \times 2200}} \text{ m} = 0.55 \text{ m}$$

Similarly, the width of the wall needed to withstand grain stacked to a height of 2 m is 0.49 m, and to a height of 1.5 m is 0.42 m. Thus the 1.06 m thickness of the Corbridge walls would be more than sufficient to withstand the pressures of grain stacked against them to a height in excess of 3 m.

APPENDIX 2

AN ATTEMPT TO ASSESS THE WEIGHT OF THE ROOF OF THE
WEST GRANARY (PHASE 4) AT CORBRIDGE

Five tegulae and six imbrices from Caerleon, in the collection of the National Museum of Wales, were weighed and measured in an attempt to estimate the average weight of a granary roof.

The average size of a tegula was found to be 55 cm long, including a 5 cm overlap; and 38 cm wide, with an average weight of 25 lbs (11.34 kg). Imbrices with the same length weighed approximately 8 lbs (3.63 kg).

Taking Corbridge as an example, the length of the building is approximately 30 m and the width 9 m. The pitch of the roof is dependent upon the roof covering. In the case of tiles the pitch must be steep enough to allow rainwater to drain successfully and 25 degrees would seem sufficient. If such a pitch is allowed, it is calculated that the length of the rafters needed would be 6 m, including an overhang which continues to the outer face of the buttresses.

Each half of the roof would need: 80 tegulae to cover the 30 m length
                                   12 tegulae to cover the 6 m rafters
                                   = 960 tegulae

In addition, a similar number of semi-circular imbrices would be necessary to cover the junctions of the tegulae = 960 imbrices.

The total number of tiles for the entire roof = 1920 tegulae + 1920 imbrices.

The approx. weight of 1920 tegulae   = 1920 x 25 lbs (11.34 kg)
                                      = 48 000 lbs (21 772 kg)

The approx. weight of 1920 imbrices   = 1920 x 8 lbs (3.63 kg)
                                      = 15 360 lbs (6 969 kg)

Total weight of tiles estimated: = 63 360 lbs (28 740 kg) = 28 tons

Although the method of roof construction of such a building is completely unknown, it is reasonable to suppose that it was similar in many respects to the simple Medieval examples, in which the tiles would have been supported by a framework of timber trusses. These timbers would take the form of a triangular frame consisting of two rafters meeting at the ridge and held rigid by means of a horizontal tie beam, and keyed into the top of the wall by longitudinal wall plates. They would have been placed at regular intervals along the length of the building, the tie beams probably supported, as in the Corbridge example, upon paired buttresses. Other longitudinal timbers would have been added to give the framework rigidity, purlins half way up the roof on each side, and a ridge piece at the apex of the rafters. Laths may have been added to give further strength, and to support the tiles. (See Fig. 1).

The tapering of the regulae exerts a lateral thrust which helps to lock the body of tiles together, on a relatively shallow pitched roof. Also, the notching of the tegulae and the nail holes present in the imbrices examined suggest that they could have been secured adequately as in Fig. 2, without mortaring, although the joints between the tiles were probably mortared to render them watertight.

Thus, in addition to the weight of the tiles, the weight of the timber roof frame must also be taken into consideration. This calculation assumes that a 30 m length of oak 9 x 6 in (229 x 152 mm) weighs 1653 lbs (750 kg). 5 x 30 m lengths would probably be needed; 2 for the wall plates, 2 for the purlins, and 1 ridge piece. Their combined weight would be:

$$5 \times 1653 \text{ lbs} = 8265 \text{ lbs } (3\ 750 \text{ kg})$$

10 tie beams would be needed, 1 upon each end wall, and eight supported by the eight intermediate buttresses, = 10 x 551 lbs (250 kg)
= 5510 lbs (2500 kg)

Also, 10 x 12 m lengths for the rafters = 10 x 660 lbs (300 kg).
= 6600 lbs (3000 kg)

Allowing an extra 4 x 30 m lengths for laths = 6600 lbs (3000 kg)

<u>Total estimated weight of timbering</u> = 26 975 lbs (12 250 kg) = <u>12 tons</u>

These calculations would give the very minimum estimated weight of the roof of one of the Corbridge granaries including both tiles and timbers as <u>40 tons.</u>

APPENDIX 3

TO DETERMINE THE SIZE OF BUTTRESSES NECESSARY TO SUPPORT A TILED ROOF OF 40 TONS WEIGHT

(Taking the west granary at Corbridge (Phase 4), as an example)

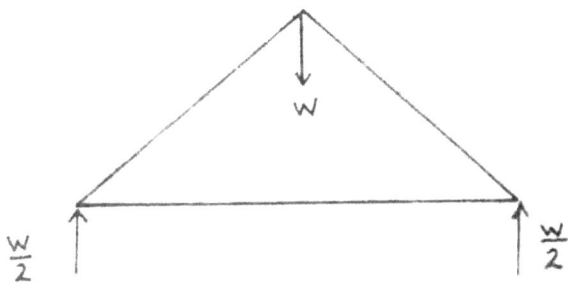

Total weight of roof = 40 tons = 40 641.88 kg.

Assume this to be equally carried by 8 roof trusses supported on pairs of buttresses.

$$W = \frac{40642}{8} = 5080 \text{ kg}$$

each reaction $\frac{W}{2} = 2540$ kg

If each support were placed vertically (without side support to prevent bending) Euler's theory of struts could be applied:

$$\frac{W}{2} = \frac{\pi^2 E I}{4 l^2}$$

Where E = Young's Elastic Modulus
I = Moment of inertia of support

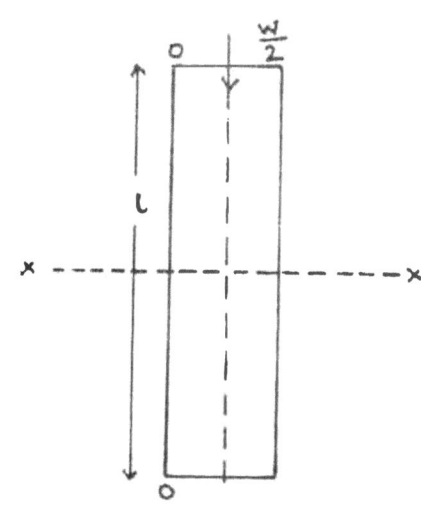

$I_{xx} = \frac{a^4}{12}$ (for square section)

also $I_{oo} = 2 I_{xx} = \frac{a^4}{6}$

$$I = \frac{4 w l^2}{2 \pi^2 E}$$

$$\frac{a^4}{6} = \frac{2 w l^2}{\pi^2 E}$$

or $a = \sqrt[4]{\frac{12 w l^2}{\pi^2 E}}$

$$a = \sqrt[4]{\frac{12 \times 5080 \times 9}{9.87 \times 75\,906}}$$

If we assume that the height of the wall is 3 m and

$E = 75\,906$ kg/m^2 (13 000 tons/in^2)

$= \underline{0.92\text{ m}}$

Thus the minimum cross section of buttresses required to support a roof weighing 40 641 kg (40 tons) = 0.92 m.

Similar calculations to determine the cross section of buttresses necessary at Castlecary

Overall length = 27.11 m   Overall breadth = 6.39 m

It is calculated that the length of the rafters = 3.52 m which would require 71 x 7 tegulae and imbrices on each side of the roof.

Tiles needed

994 tegulae weighing 25 lbs each = 24850 lbs = 11.09 tons (11281 kg)
994 imbrices   "   8 lbs each = 7952 lbs = 3.55 tons (3610 kg)

Total weight of tiles = 14.6 tons (14 891 kg)
Total weight of timbers = approx. 9.3 tons (9457 kg)
Weight of roof calculated = $\underline{23.9 \text{ tons}} = 24\,283.5$ kg
W = distributed by 10 pairs of buttresses = $\frac{24283}{10}$ = 2428 kg

$$a = \sqrt[4]{\frac{12 \times 2428 \times 9}{9.87 \times 75\,906}}$$

$a = \underline{0.77\text{ m}}$

APPENDIX 4

SIZES AND PROPORTIONS OF SINGLE GRANARIES

Name of Fort	Length	Breadth	Proportions
Balmuildy (w)	25.60 m	8.23 m	3.1 : 1
(e)	26.21 m	6.71 m	3.9 : 1
Bar Hill	25.90 m	9.75 m	2.7 : 1
Birrens (w)	21.10 m	7.38 m	2.9 : 1
(e)	22.93 m	7.38 m	3.1 : 1
Cadder (n)	20.12 m	6.10 m	3.3 : 1
(s)	20.12 m	6.71 m	3.0 : 1
Caernarfon (both)	29.25 m	7.61 m	3.8 : 1
Caersws II	28.95 m	10.20 m	2.8 : 1
Camelon	32.31 m	6.10 m	5.3 : 1
Cappuck	15.85 m	6.10 m	2.6 : 1
Castell Collen	28.34 m	9.75 m	2.9 : 1
Castlecary	27.11 m	6.39 m	4.2 : 1
Chester	48.46 m	13.41 m	3.6 : 1
Corbridge (w)	29.87 m	9.14 m	3.3 : 1
(Phase 3/4) (e)	28.04 m	9.75 m	2.9 : 1
(Site XI)	19.80 m	7.50 m	2.6 : 1
Crawford II	21.34 m	6.71 m	3.2 : 1
Croy Hill	14.12 m	5.28 m	2.7 : 1
Gelligaer II (both)	18.59 m	9.45 m	2.0 : 1
Haltonchesters	41.15 m	10.36 m	4.0 : 1
Haltwhistle Burn	11.96 m	9.15 m	1.3 : 1
Ilkley	23.78 m	9.14 m	2.6 : 1
Lyne	29.56 m	6.10 m	4.8 : 1
Mumrills (w)	30.02 m	6.91 m	4.3 : 1
(e)	30.07 m	6.55 m	4.6 : 1
Newstead (both)	37.49 m	10.66 m	3.5 : 1
Old Kilpatrick	26.20 m	7.61 m	3.4 : 1
Rough Castle	22.09 m	6.24 m	3.5 : 1
Rudchester	37.32 m	9.13 m	4.1 : 1
Stanwix	36.58 m	9.14 m	4.0 : 1
South Shields (Severan)	29.89 m	6.10 m	4.9 : 1

FOOTNOTES

1. See Rickman, 1971, 251.
2. Manning, 1975, 105-129.
3. Coope and Osborne, 1967, 84-87 and Osborne, 1971, 162-4; who also records that the saw-toothed grain beetle was detected in the tomb of Tutankhamen and at Herculaneum (dal Monte, 1956).
4. Armstrong and Howe, 1963, 256-261.
5. Oxley, 1948, 24.
6. Solomon and Adamson, 1955, 311-355.
7. Coombs and Freeman, 1955, 399-417.
8. H.M.S.O. 1966, 134.
9. De Agric. XCII.
10. Res Rusticae LVII.
11. Ibid., LXIII.
12. De Archit. VI, VI, 4.
13. De Re Rust. I, vi, 9-17.
14. Ibid., II, xx, 6.
15. Nat. Hist. XVIII, 302.
16. Rickman, 1971, 221.
17. Niederbieber, ORL Lief LV Nr Ia, 25 and Weissenburg ORL Lief XXXI Nr 31, 31. See also Rickman, 1971, 241-2.
18. Jones and Little, 1973, 11.
19. Frere, 1967, 124.
20. Jarrett, 1969, 51, 69 and 62.
21. Rickman, 1971, 241-244.
22. Curle, 1911.
23. Clarke, 1933.
24. Richmond and Gillam, 1950, 153.
25. Ward, 1903, 62-3.
26. Curle, 1911.

27. Similarly, although they have not yet been located, it seems likely that the granaries of the legionary fortress of Caerleon were conveniently situated near the south-west gate to give easy access to the wharves on the River Usk. See Boon. *Isca*. 1972, 122 (note 14).

28. *Curr. Arch.* 50, May 1975. 88 and information from Dr. D. J. Breeze.

29. See page 2.

30. I am grateful to Mr. R. W. Howe of the Pest Infestation Control Laboratory for pointing this out.

31. See Rickman, 1971, 236.

32. Bulmer, 1969, 10.

33. See note in *JRS* 51 (1961), 158.

34. Philp, 1973 and *Curr. Arch.* 38, May 1973, 86.

35. Richmond and Gillam, 1950, 157.

36. Davies, 1971.

37. Haverfield and Collingwood, 1920, 127.

38. Richmond and McIntyre, 1939.

39. Bulmer, 1969, 9.

40. Jacobi, 1914, 75-95.

41. Weisbaden, Ritterling, *Nass Mitt* 1901-2. Part 2, 56. Mainz, Korber, *Rom. Insc. von Mainz* III, 1897, No. 84.

42. Jacobi, 1914, 90 and Moritz, 1958, 126.

43. Richmond and McIntyre, 1939.

44. Hogg, 1968, and Robertson, 1975, 20.

45. Haverfield and Collingwood, 1920, 140 and Bulmer, 1969, 7.

46. Polybius, *Histories* VI, 39, 12.

47. Cicero, *In Verr.* iii, 45, 46, 49.

48. Smith, 1849, 748.

49. Fink, 1971, 78 1, 2 & 3; 79 and 81.

50. Smith, 1849, 137.

51. Haverfield, 1916,

52. Pliny, *Nat. Hist.* XVIII, 67. For further information on the extraction rates of flour in the Classical world see Jasny, 1944 and Moritz, 1958, 184-215.

53. Fink, 1971, 78, 79 and 81.

54. H.M.S.O. 1971, 48.

55. Weller, 1965, Vol. 1.

56. Agricola XII, 2. Haverfield and Collingwood, 1920, 140.

57. SHA Hadrianus 10, 2. 'cibis etiam castrensibus in propatulo libenter utens, hoc est larido, caseo et posca.'

58. Plaut. Capt. iv, 4.6. Pliny, Nat. Hist. XVIII, 60.

59. Davies, 1971.

60. Helbaek, 1964, 158.

61. St. Joesph, 1951, 53.

62. Simpson and Richmond, 1941, 18. The actual length of the building could not be ascertained because the praetentura and via principalis lay under a reservoir. It is possible that the excavators overestimated the length of the granary, thus distorting the amount of floor area available for storage.

63. McKay, 1971, 99.

64. H.M.S.O. 1971, 48.

65. Breeze and Dobson, 1969, 15-32; 1973, 109-121; 1974, 13-20.

66. See Breeze and Dobson, 1959, 24 which includes the suggestion by Mr. J. P. Gillam that the granaries at Haltonchesters and Rudchester display such similarities in construction with Benwell that they may all have been built by the same unit, namely a detachment of the fleet. See Gillam, 1961a, 6.

67. The plans shown in fig. 9 are my own based upon the original in Richmond and Gillam, 1950, and are therefore only approximations.

68. Associated with this period was a row of stake holes, along the outer face of the west wall of the east granary, which may have functioned structurally in a half-timbered building, although interpretation of these features presents difficulties. Mr. Gillam points out that similar stake holes have been detected alongside several other buildings of the Period IVa fort, where they occur only in association with sill beams or stone walls, and are thus not exclusive to the granaries.

69. Brassington, 1975, 66.

70. Ibid., 68.

71. Richmond and Gillam, 1950, 157.

72. Ministry of Works, 1952.

73. Ibid., 17.

74. loc. cit.

75. Manning, 1975, 129.

76. Compare with posts alongside Corbridge east granary, note 68 above.
77. Hartley, 1958.
78. Richmond, 1934, 83-103.
79. Ibid., 101.
80. Birley, 1961, 207.
81. Frere, 1967, 124

INDEX

Access 4, 7, 13
Aerial photography 59, 60, 95
Amphorae 26
Amurca 5
Annual grain requirement 25, 28

Bins (storage) 18
Birds 3
Bread 24
Bricks 6
Buttresses 7, 15, 16, 39, 55

Capacity 25, 28
Cavalry 27
Charred grain 26, 27
Clay floors 9
Construction 7
Contubernia 20, 28
Corn dryers 58, 82

Dates of construction 7
Daily grain ration 23, 25
Diet (military) 26
Doors 11, 13
Double granaries 7
Drainage 13
Dunnage 15

Eaves 3
Epigraphic evidence 23

Flagging 9
Fleet 59
Floors 9
Floor area, as % of fort area 27, 30, 31
Floor supports 8
Flour 25
Foundations 4, 8
Fungus 2

Garrisons, see catalogue entries
Grain mills 20
Granary weevil 2

Harbour 14
Height, surviving and conjectured 16

Individual granaries (structural features)
    - see catalogue
Infestation 3
Internal layout 18
Insects 2
Inscriptions - see catalogue

Lateral thrust of grain 4, 15, 35
Lead seals 92, 94
Loading 4
Loading platforms 12

Measures 23
Meat 16
Moisture content of grain 3
Mullions 75

Nails 84

Oak boards 57
Oil 5
Opus signinum 5
Ovens 20

Pillars 10
Planks 10
Porticos 12
Proportions 7, 41
Provisions 26

Querns 20

Rations 23
Rebuilding 10, 11
Reconstruction (suggested) 17
Reserve supplies 27, 28
Rodents 3, 11
Roof (construction and weight) 16, 37

Sacks 18, 20
Sandstone roofing 80
Second storeys 16
Siting 13
Size 7, 41
Sleeper walls 9
Staircases 16
Steps 13

Structural requirements 4

Temperature control 3, 15
Tiles 15, 16, 19, 37
Timber granary 34
Timber in granary construction 16, 38
Transit granaries 18, 28
Transport of grain 18
Transverse walls 8

Variations (in design) 7
Vegetables 26
Ventilation 3
Ventilators 11

Walls 7, 8, 55
Wall plaster 5, 81
Wicker basket 18
Weight of grain 25
Wine 26

ROMAN MILITARY STONE-BUILT GRANARIES IN BRITAIN

PART II: CATALOGUE OF EXCAVATED EXAMPLES

INTRODUCTION

The plans have been drawn to a uniform scale of 1:400 and they are orientated so that the via principalis is at the lower end of the plan. Foundations have been stippled.

In the sections on garrisons I have relied heavily upon the advice of Dr. M. G. Jarrett and three papers by D. J. Breeze and B. Dobson concerned with fort types and garrisons[65] Where possible the dimensions quoted are those taken from the text of the excavation report and converted into metric units, but in cases where they were omitted it has been necessary to calculate them from the published plan, which may lead to some unavoidable inaccuracies. Details of the thickness of external walls, the sizes of buttresses and their spacing have been tabulated below (Table 4, p. 55).

The location of all the sites mentioned are shown in Map 1, and those situated in the frontier region are shown in more detail in Map 2.

KEY TO NUMBERED FORTS IN MAPS 1 AND 2

1.	Old Kilpatrick	44.	Slack
2.	New Kilpatrick	45.	Doncaster
3.	Balmuildy	46.	Templeborough
4.	Cadder	47.	Brough on Noe
5.	Bar Hill	48.	Caernarfon
6.	Croy Hill	49.	Caerhun
7.	Castlecary	50.	Chester
8.	Rough Castle	51.	Caersws II
9.	Camelon	52.	Buckton
10.	Mumrills	53.	Castell Collen
11.	Cramond	54.	Pumpsaint
12.	Inveresk	55.	Beulah
13.	Castledykes	56.	Brecon Gaer
14.	Lyne	57.	Penydarren
15.	Crawford II	58.	Gelligaer II
16.	Newstead	59.	Dover
17.	Cappuck		
18.	High Rochester		
19.	Birrens		
20.	Drumburgh		
21.	Stanwix		
22.	Old Church, Brampton		
23.	Birdoswald		
24.	Great Chesters		
25.	Haltwhistle Burn		
26.	Housesteads		
27.	Chesters		
28.	Haltonchesters		
29.	Corbridge		
30.	Rudchester		
31.	Benwell		
32.	South Shields		
33.	Beckfoot		
34.	Old Penrith		
35.	Whitley Castle		
36.	Chester-le-Street		
37.	Hardknott.		
38.	Ambleside		
39.	Watercrook		
40.	Brough by Bainbridge		
41.	Lancaster		
42.	Ilkley		
43.	Ribchester		

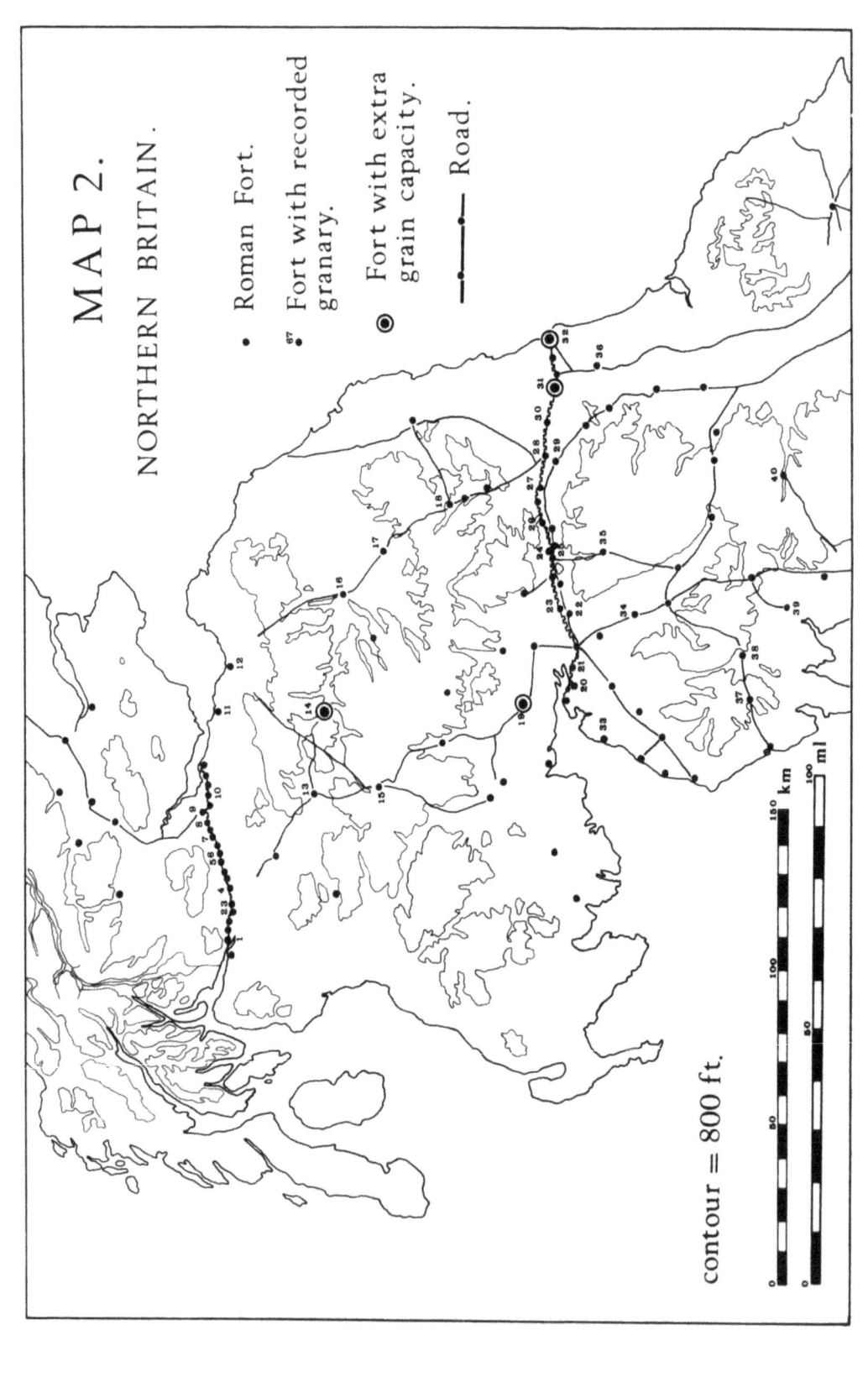

TABLE 4

DIMENSIONS OF EXTERNAL WALLS AND BUTTRESSES

Name of Fort	External walls Thickness (m)	Buttresses Width and projection	No. of pairs	Distance apart(m)
Ambleside	0.91	0.91 m square	7	n) 2.13 s) 2.44
Balmuildy	0.91	0.76 m square	8	2.40
Bar Hill	0.61	none	-	-
Benwell	1.22	1.22 x 0.61 m	?	2.54
Birdoswald	0.91	1.06 m square	9	2.30
Birrens (w)	1.10	1.2-1.5 m square	9	1.22-1.5
(e)	1.10	approx. 1 m square	9	1.80?
(double)	0.86	0.91 m square	13	2.10
Brecon Gaer	1.22	0.76 m square	10	2.30
Cadder	1.06(founds)	approx. 1 m square	6	2.44
Caerhun	1.06	0.76 m square	8	2.28
Caernarfon	0.91	none	-	-
Caer Sws II	0.91	0.91 m square	7	4?
Camelon	0.91	approx. 0.91 m square	11	2.15?
Cappuck	1.22	approx. 1.22 m square	7	1.50
Castell Collen	1.37	0.76 x 0.61 m	11	2.13
Castlecary	0.91	0.76 m square	10	2.18
Castledykes	1.83-1.30	1 only, projecting 0.91	?	?
Chester	1.01	0.91 m square	17?	2.06
Chester le Street	1.52	0.91 m square	?	2.89
Corbridge (e+w)	1.06	approx 0.91 m square	8	2.10
Cramond (w)	0.91	0.91 m square	?	3?
(e)	0.68	0.91 m square	?	3?
Crawford	0.91	approx. 1 m square	?	?
Croy Hill	0.81	0.91 m square	6	1.83
Drumburgh	0.81	0.81 m square	?	3.05
Gelligaer II (w)	1.22	0.61 m square	8	2.44
(e)	1.22	0.61 m square	7	1.83
Great Chesters	0.90	approx. 0.90 m square	?	?
Haltwhistle	0.61	0.76 x 0.84 m	6 (west)	0.90
Hardknott	1.06	0.76 m square	5	3.05
High Rochester	1.06	0.76 m square	8	2.44
Housesteads	0.91	0.91 m square	7	3.20
Ilkley	1.06-1.22	1.06 m square	?	?
Lyne (single)	1.06-1.22	1.22 m square	12	1.22?
(double)	1.06-1.22	0.91 m square	12(s)	1.22?
Mumrills	1.22	0.91 m square	13	1.52
Newstead (s)	0.76	1.06 m square	?	2.13-2.44
(n)	0.76	0.76 m square	?	2.13-2.44

Old Church	0.91	?	?	?
Old Kilpatrick	1.06	0.76 x 0.91 m	11	1.78
Penydarren	0.76	approx. 0.76 m square	?	3.05
Pumpsaint	0.90?	approx. 1 m x 1.20 m	?	3.20?
Ribchester	0.76	?	11	1.80-2.45
Rough Castle	0.76	0.61 m square	9	2.13?
Rudchester	1.06	1.06 m x 0.61 m	10-11	2.74
Slack	0.91	none	-	-
South Shields (Had.)			10	
(Sev.)			10	
Stanwix	0.90?	?	?	?
Templeborough	0.91	0.91 x 0.76 m	?	2.13

AMBLESIDE   Cumbria, NY 3703

Overall area, 1.22 ha; 1.04 ha. within ramparts

References   Collingwood, 1915

Garrison   Probably a <u>cohors quingenaria</u>

Granaries   One double granary in the central range between the principia
(fig. 6)   and the north gate, at right angles to the via principalis. Un-
               certain date.

    Dimensions - 20.12 x 20.12 m overall; internally the northern half - 18.29 x 5.49 m and the south - 18.29 x 7.01 m, giving a total floor area of 228.6 sq m. Constructed with local Brathay stone. The foundations consisted of large stones laid diagonally in clay, and overlain by flagstones. The floor was supported on longitudinal sleeper walls, 0.61 m wide and 1.80 m apart in the northern part, and 0.76 - 0.91 m wide and approx 1 m apart in the south. The wide spacing of the sleeper walls implies a timber floor. Ventilators were present between the buttresses on the north and south walls, with one on the east; those on the north were parallel sided, and those on the south and east splayed inwards.

    Slate from the roof was found within the building. A central space between the two granaries contained the remains of three transverse walls. On the east side were traces of burning and a quantity of charred wheat upon oak boards, suggested by the excavator as the remains of a burnt bin; more probably floorboards.

Structural   Differences in the ventilators and the absence of freestone
alterations   in the buttresses of the south wall suggest modification.

BALMUILDY   Lanarkshire, NS 5871

Overall area, 1.75 ha; 1.32 ha. within ramparts

References   Miller, 1922

Garrison   Possibly a <u>cohors quingenaria equitata</u>

Granaries   Two single granaries in the central range on either side of the
(fig. 6)   principia, at right angles to the via principalis. Antonine.

    Dimensions - east) 26.21 x 6.71 m overall; 24.39 x 4.89m internally, west) 25.60 x 8.23 m overall; 23.78 x 6.41 m internally, giving a total floor area of 271.7 sq m. The foundations consisted of clay and cobbles extending to the outer face of the buttresses. The floor was supported in both granaries upon three longitudinal sleeper walls approx. 1.20 m apart; this distance suggests timber flooring. A single ventilator survived in the east wall of the east granary, between the 4th and 5th buttresses; splaying inwards from 23-45 cm.

A possible loading platform between two buttresses on the south wall of the east granary was suggested by the excavator. Iron nails, roofing tiles, amphora and glass fragments were associated with the granaries.

Structural alterations
A kiln was inserted in the north end of the east granary at an unknown date.

BAR HILL Dunbarton, NS 7075

Overall area, 1.37 ha; 1.29 ha. within ramparts

References Macdonald, 1906. Robertson, Scott and Keppie, 1975

Garrison Probably a <u>cohors quingenaria peditata</u>. Coh. I Baetasiorum is attested in the Antonine period. (RIB 2169, 2170). Three timber barracks were identified in the retentura containing 10 contubernia.

Granaries (fig. 6)
One double granary in the central range next to and north-east of the principia, at right angles to the via principalis. Antonine.

Dimensions - 25.90 x 9.75 m overall and 24.68 x 8.53 m internally, giving a floor area of 210.5 sq m. The foundations consisted of clay with cobbles. The floor, presumably timber, was supported in the western half by 3 irregularly spaced longitudinal sleeper walls, whilst the eastern half was paved at ground level. No buttresses are recorded in the excavation report, although a photograph of the excavation appears to show at least one.

A stone gutter ran parallel with the west side of the granary, approx. 1.20 m from the external wall. A 'good many ashes' were recorded in the northern part of the granary in the space between the sleeper walls; possibly the remains of burnt flooring.

Structural alterations
It is possible that the plan shows the latest phase of modification, and that the longitudinal sleeper walls with timber flooring originally occupied the entire building.

BEARSDEN Dunbarton, NS 545721

Overall area, 1.2 ha; 1.1 ha. within ramparts

References Breeze, 1974 and 1975

Garrison Five timber blocks excavated; one with a central drain which suggests stabling. Barracks contained 8 contubernia.

Granaries Fragmentary traces of one granary situated next to the north-west gate, parallel with the via principalis. Antonine.

17.7 m of the north wall was uncovered. The floor was probably supported upon sleeper walls.

BECKFOOT   Cumbria, NY 0848

Internal area approx. 1 ha. + (from aerial photograph)

References   St. Joseph, 1951, 56

Garrison   Probably a <u>cohors quingenaria peditata.</u> Coh. II Pannoniorum is attested by <u>RIB</u> 880, probably during the second century. 6 barracks visible in the retentura.

Granaries   The internal fort layout has been revealed by aerial photography. Two single buttressed granaries were detected: one within the central range next to the south gate, and the second parallel with it, but on the opposite side of the via principalis.

BENWELL   Tyne and Wear, NZ 2164

Overall area approx. 2.24 ha; approx 1.84 ha. within ramparts

References   Simpson and Richmond, 1941

Garrison   Probably an <u>ala quingenaria</u> under Hadrian. No Hadrianic garrison attested. A double barrack block in the retentura contained 9 contubernia, and two double blocks have been interpreted as stables. The praetentura has been destroyed by a reservoir.

Granaries (fig. 6)   One double granary in the central range next to and north west of the principia, at right angles to the via principalis. Hadrianic. <u>RIB</u> 1340 records the construction by a detachment of the fleet in Britain under Aulus Platorius Nepos A.D. 122-126.[66] This inscription came from the centre of the granary portico, lying face downwards, and shattered by its fall.

Dimensions - overall estimated length 45.72 x 18.29 m; and internally estimated 43.28 x 6.86 m (eastern part), and 7.32 m west, giving a total estimated floor area of 613.7 sq m. The foundations consisted of clay and rubble pitched herring-bone-wise, 0.61 m deep overlain by stone flagging.

The east granary was entered by a flight of steps 2.89 m broad. A portico consisting of 6 rectangular piers on splayed bases fronted the granaries.

BEULAH   Powys, SN 923502

Overall area, 1.7 ha; reduced to 1.2 ha.

References   Jones, G.D.B. and Birley, A.R. 1966

Granaries   One single granary at the northern end of the central range. Possibly Trajanic.

Very few details of this granary are known. The overall width was 11.6 m and the floor was supported upon small stone pillars.

BIRDOSWALD Cumbria, NY 6166

Overall area, c. 2.15 ha; 1.88 ha. within ramparts

References Bruce, 1860. Simpson and Richmond, 1931

Garrison Probably a cohors milliaria peditata under Hadrian. Coh. I Aelia Dacorum is attested in the third century. (RIB 1872 etc.) One barrack with ten contubernia located, the remainder not fully excavated. No stables recorded.

Granaries Two single granaries have been revealed by aerial photography, (St. Joseph, 1951, 55), one of which has been partly excavated. Situated within the central range, west of the principia, parallel with the via principalis. Hadrianic, rebuilt A.D. 205-8; RIB 1909 records the completion of a granary in the governorship of Alfenus Senecio by coh. I Aelia Dacorum and coh. I Thracum.

Dimensions - 28.04 x ? m overall; 26.20 x ? m internally. (The granary could be as much as 15.24 m wide). A stone flagged floor was supported upon longitudinal walls. Narrow ventilators were present between the buttresses on the long wall.

Stone roofing slabs, many with nail holes were associated with the granary.

BIRRENS Dumfries, NY 2175

Overall area, 1.97 ha; 1.65 ha. within ramparts

References Christison, 1895. Birley, 1938. Robertson, 1975.

Garrison Probably a cohors milliaria equitata in the Antonine period. Garrison of the Antonine I fort attested as Coh. I Nervana Germanorum (JRS 1964, 178 no. 6, and RIB 2093). Four pairs of barracks revealed in the praetentura, and six pairs in the retentura; also six single buildings interpreted as stables/stores. There seems to have been no alteration in the fort size or accommodation in Antonine II, which probably contained the same size of unit, perhaps Coh. II Tungrorum (cf. RIB 2092 and 2110).

Granaries (fig. 6) Two single granaries in the central range, one immediately west of the principia, and the other next to the east gate; both at right angles to the via principalis. The double granary lay on the opposite side of the via principalis and parallel with it, also next to the east gate. Antonine.

Dimensions - singles. West) 21.10 x 7.38 m overall, 18.90 x 5.18 m internally; east) 22.93 x 7.38 m overall, and 20.73 x 5.18 m internally, giving a total floor area of 205.3 sq m. Double - 36.60 x 9.75 m overall; the western part 16.76 x 7.93 m internally and the eastern, 17.35 x

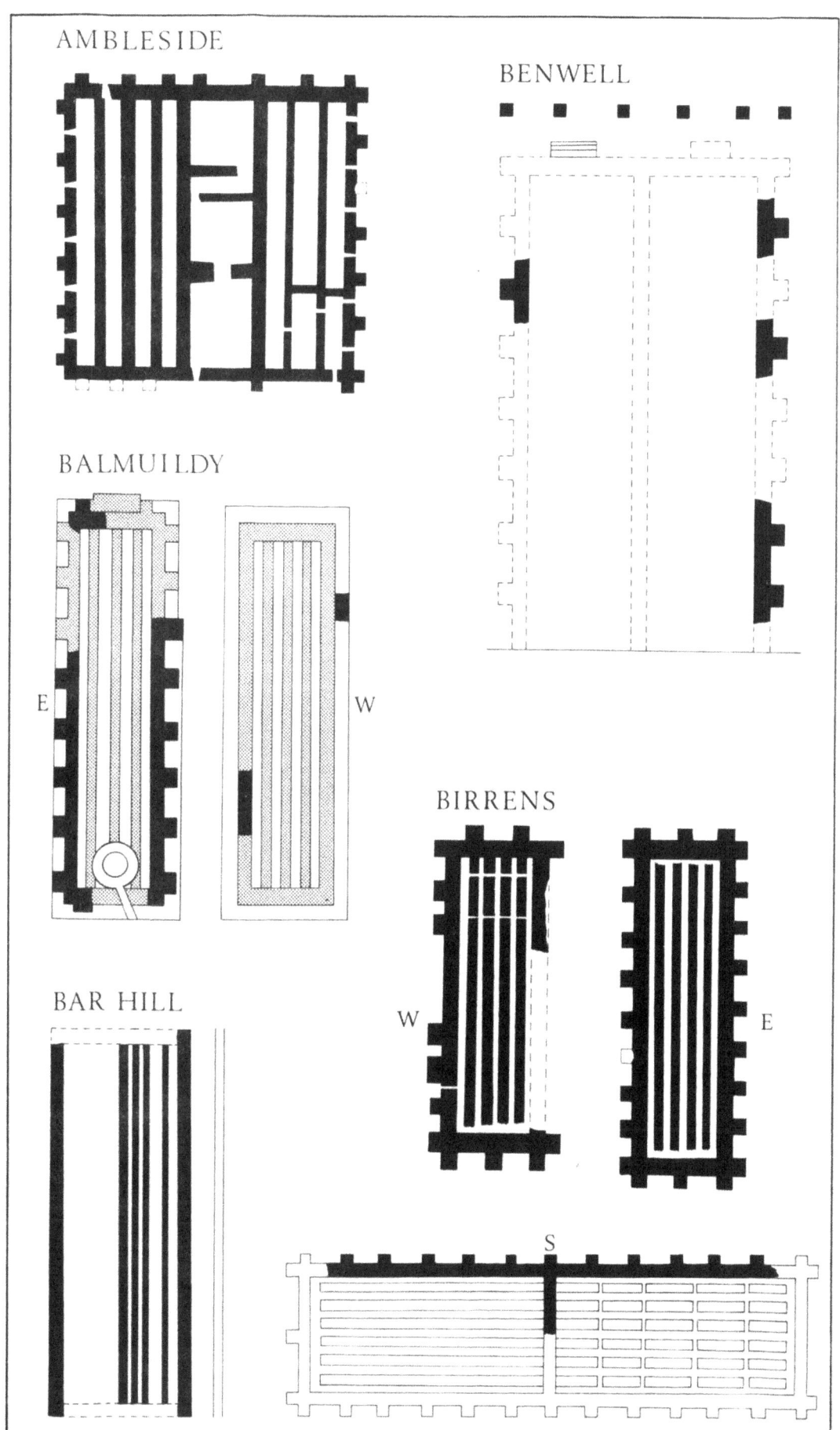

Fig. 6

7.93 internally, giving a total floor area of 270.5 sq m. The total floor area available for grain storage in all three granaries - 475.8 sq m. The floor was supported upon longitudinal sleeper walls; 4 in the singles, and 6 in the double granary, all pierced at regular intervals. The method of flooring is unknown. Only one ventilator survived, in the west wall of the west granary.

Drains were located to the east and west of the double granary. A quantity of calcined wheat was found in the west granary, and soot was found between the floor supports of the double granary.

BRECON GAER   Powys, SO 0029

Overall area, 3.14 ha; 2.57 ha. within ramparts.

References	Wheeler, 1926a, 1926b. Jarrett, 1968.
Garrison	Probably an ala quingenaria at first; cf. RIB 403, which attests the ala Hispanorum Vettonum civium Romanorum in late 1st-2nd century. Later reduced.
Granaries (fig. 7)	One double granary in the central range between the principia and the north-west gate, at right angles to the via principalis. Constructed after c. A.D. 140, which is the earliest date for stone structures here.

Dimensions - 29.26 x 14.0 m overall; each half 27.0 x 5.0 m internally, giving a total floor area of 270 sq m. The granary had a rough flagged floor at ground level.

BROUGH BY BAINBRIDGE   North Yorkshire, SD 9390

References	Wade, 1952
Granaries	The north-west corner of the principia was examined in 1951. It was found that the north wall was constructed upon the foundations of an earlier granary wall. Its surviving foundations had two buttresses 9.14 m apart.

A quantity of carbonised wheat and barley was discovered in this foundation trench, but no dating evidence was recovered.

BROUGH ON NOE   Derbyshire, SK 1882

Overall area, 0.8 ha.

References	Sheffield University, 1959. Jones and Wild, 1967-9.
Garrison	Possibly a cohors quingenaria. Fragmentary traces of Severan timber barracks were replaced by six stone barracks and stables in the final period of occupation.
Granaries (fig. 7)	In 1958 a granary was located within the central range between the principia and the north-west gate, at right angles

to the via principalis. The results of this excavation are largely unpublished.

Excavations in 1967-9 revealed traces of another stone granary overlying a post-built Antonine predecessor, to the north east of the principia. The suggested reconstruction by the excavator shows a structure 21.30 x 9.14 m with transverse sleeper walls. It seems equally possible that the surviving walls represent the external walls and longitudinal sleeper walls of a large structure at right angles to the via principalis, and stretching back as far as the via quintana.

A drain which originally served the underlying timber granary may have been retained.

BUCKTON   Hereford and Worcester. SO 390733

References   St. Joseph, 1961.

Garrison   Details of the fort's layout became apparent from aerial photographs taken during the drought of 1959. The size and detail so far revealed seem to be appropriate to a cohors milliaria. A section cut through the eastern defences, and examination of the east gate, has suggested a date in the first half of the second century for the occupation of this fort.

Granaries   One granary was detected in the central range of stone buildings, to the south of the principia.

CADDER   Lanark, NS 6172

Overall area, 1.34 ha; 1.15 ha. within ramparts

References   Clarke, 1933

Garrison   Probably a cohors quingenaria, possibly equitata. Four barracks were located in the retentura, and two in the praetentura; also two possible stables in the retentura, although this is less certain.

Granaries (fig. 7)   Two single granaries in the central range on either side of the principia, at right angles to the via principalis. Antonine.

Dimensions - north) 20.12 x 6.10 m overall, 18.0 x 4.25 m internally; south) 20.12 x 6.71 m overall, 18.0 x 4.60 m internally, giving a total floor area of 159.3 sq m. The foundations consisted of clay and cobbles. The flooring was supported upon longitudinal sleeper walls; the remains of one was found in the south granary.

The area between the front of each granary and the via principalis was heavily cobbled, which may suggest the foundations of loading platforms. A flue which passed through the west wall of the north granary was thought by Macdonald (1934) to be the remnant of a corn drying kiln.

CAERHUN   Gwynedd, SH 7770

Overall area, 1.97 ha; 1.60 ha. within ramparts

References   Reynolds, 1938

Garrison   Possibly a <u>cohors quingenaria equitata.</u> Five pairs of barracks; and two long buildings in the retentura which may represent stables.

Granaries (fig. 7)   One double granary in the central range between the principia and the north gate, at right angles to the via principalis. Probably Antonine.

Dimensions - 22.69 x 27.43 m overall; each part 20.57 x 6.86 m internally, giving a total floor area of 282.2 sq m. The foundations were packed carefully with puddled blue clay. The floor consisted of mixed clay with traces of 3-7 cm thick decomposed pink cement at the east and west ends.

Against the south wall of the south granary, between the 3rd and 5th buttresses was a large quantity of stone, suggested by the excavator as a loading platform. A gutter running across the central courtyard from east to west was revealed by silt 0.12 m deep and 0.76 m wide, which continued east of the granary wall. The enclosing walls of the courtyard area between the two granaries appear to be contemporary; the floor was also clay.

CAERNARFON   Gwynedd, SH 4862

Overall area, 2.27 ha; 1.97 ha. within ramparts

References   Wheeler, 1922 and 1924

Garrison   Probably a <u>cohors milliaria.</u> Six barracks are known in the retentura and 5/6 in the praetentura.

Granaries (fig. 7)   Two single granaries in the central range next to and east of the principia, parallel with the via principalis. Probably constructed after A.D. 140.

Dimensions - both 29.25 x 7.61 m overall; 27.43 x 5.79 m internally, giving a total floor area of 317.6 sq m. Constructed exclusively of Chester stone. A clay floor survived in the south granary. Unbuttressed.

Next to the north gate was a long building, buttressed along its northern side; its exact dimensions could not be ascertained. The excavator suggested that this may have served as an additional store.

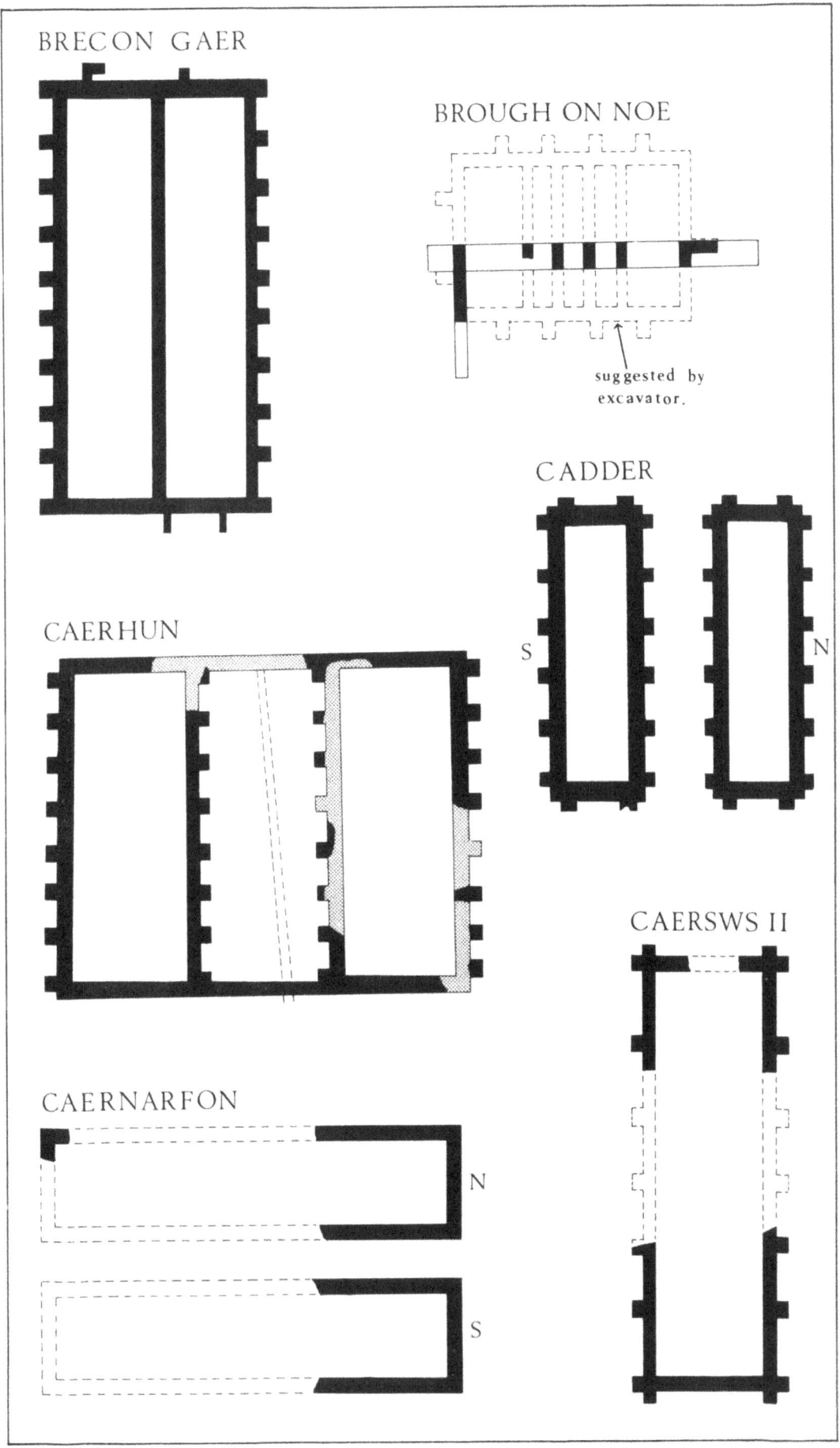

Fig. 7

Structural alterations	Two rough buttresses were added to the south granary. Also a small external chamber 1.50 m square, constructed from reused material, was added to the eastern angle of the north granary.

CAERSWS II   Powys, SO 0292

Overall area, 3.11 ha; 2.50 ha within ramparts.

References	Pryce, 1940. Daniels et al., 1966-7.
Garrison	Possibly an ala quingenaria. Tile stamps of coh. I Celtiberians are attested (CIL vii 1243). Only fragmentary traces of timber barracks are known.
Granaries (Fig. 7)	One single granary in the central range, east of the principia, at right angles to the via principalis. Late Hadrianic-Antonine.

Dimensions - 26.82 x 9.50 m overall; 24.38 x 7.01 m internally, giving a floor area of 170.9 sq. m. Constructed of local freestone. A flagged floor resting upon 0.20 m clay was preserved on the eastern side.

Roofing tiles, both tegulae and imbrices were associated with this granary.

Structural alterations	The flagged floor much split by fires may indicate reuse as living quarters.

CAMELON   Stirling, NS 8681

Overall area, 3.69 ha; 2.41 ha within ramparts.

References	Buchanan, 1900.
Garrison	Eight barrack blocks in the praetentura; the retentura not fully excavated.
Granaries (Fig. 8)	One single granary in the central range, next to and north of the principia, at right angles to the via principalis. Antonine.

Dimensions - 32.31 x 6.10 m overall; 30.48 x 4.27 m internally, giving a floor area of 130.2 sq m. The foundations consisted of boulders bedded in yellow clay. The floor was supported upon longitudinal sleeper walls; the type of floor is unknown.

To the south of the principia, in the central range, was a similar building with two buttresses on the east wall and a transverse sleeper wall surviving in the interior, at a depth of 0.91 m below the external walls. It seems probable that although this building differed in shape and size from that on the north side, it is nevertheless a twin granary. Dimensions - 31.09 x 10.05 m overall; 29.27 x 8.23 m internally, giving a floor area of 240.9 sq. m.

CAPPUCK   Roxburgh, NT 6921

Overall area, 0.60 ha; 0.50 ha within ramparts.

References   Stevenson and Miller, 1912.

Garrison   Probably too small for a full cohort.

Granaries   One single granary in the central range, next to and east of
(Fig. 8)   the principia, at right angles to the via principalis. Uncertain
        date.

        Dimensions - 15.24 x 6.10 m overall; 12.80 x 3.66 m internally, giving a floor area of 46.9 sq m. Constructed white sandstone upon foundations of clay and cobbles. The method of floor support and type of flooring are unknown. Ventilators were present between the buttresses on the long walls.

        The remains of a possible loading platform were located at the south end. A drain ran parallel with the east wall at a distance of approx. 1.50 m.

CASTELL COLLEN   Powys, SO 0562

Overall area, 2.34 ha; 2.09 ha within ramparts. Reduced to 1.77 ha overall; 1.46 ha within ramparts.

References   Evelyn-White, 1914.

Garrison   Probably either a <u>cohors milliaria peditata</u> or <u>cohors quingenaria equitata</u>. No garrison is attested.

Granaries   One single granary in the central range, next to and north-
(Fig. 8)   east of the principia, parallel with the via principalis. Uncertain date, but it may belong to the reduced fort, which is probably Severan.

        Dimensions - 28.34 x 9.75 m overall; 25.60 x 7.01 m internally, giving a floor area of 179.5 sq m. Constructed in dry stone masonry. The floor was supported upon transverse sleeper walls varying in thickness 0.50-0.70 m, and 0.76 m apart; the type of flooring is unknown. Ventilators were present between the buttresses on the long walls, splaying slightly outwards from 30-35 cm.

        Strong signs of burning on the outside of the 2nd ventilator from the south angle on the south-west side of the building were interpreted by the excavator as having been caused by fire issuing from the ventilator. A large quantity of wheat was found within this granary.

Structural   In some cases the sleeper wall foundations block the ventila-
alterations   tors, which were roughly infilled with stones.

CASTLECARY   Stirling, NS 7978

Overall area, 1.58 ha; 1.48 ha within ramparts.

References	Buchanan, 1903.
Garrison	Probably a cohors milliaria equitata. Coh. I Tungrorum is attested in the Antonine period. (RIB 2155).
Granaries (Fig. 8)	One single granary in the central range next to and east of the principia, at right angles to the via principalis. Antonine.

    Dimensions - 27.11 x 6.39 m overall; 25.29 x 4.57 m internally, giving a floor area of 115.6 sq m. Large boulders 31-46 cm in size, arranged in two rows supported, presumably, a timber floor. Ventilators were present between the central 3rd, 4th and 5th buttresses in the long walls; splaying inwards from 15 cm to 76 cm.

    The width of the south wall was increased over the buttresses to 1.52 m probably to accommodate a loading platform.

    There may have been a second granary parallel with this example, with the same dimensions, but no buttresses. An apsidal structure was built into the east wall.

Structural alterations	A wide doorway had originally existed in the south wall, but subsequently the whole of the front was built up flush with the face of the buttresses.

CASTLEDYKES   Lanarkshire, NS 9244

Overall area, 3.69 ha; 2.46 ha within ramparts.

References	Robertson, 1964.
Garrison	Unknown.
Granaries	One single granary in central range, next to and east of the principia, at right angles to the via principalis. Antonine.

    Dimensions - 30.48 x 13.70 (north end) and 14.63 m (south) overall; 27.88 x 10.90 m approx. internally, giving a floor area of approx. 303.9 sq m. The foundations consisted of clay and cobbles. A thick growth of trees prevented examination of the interior.

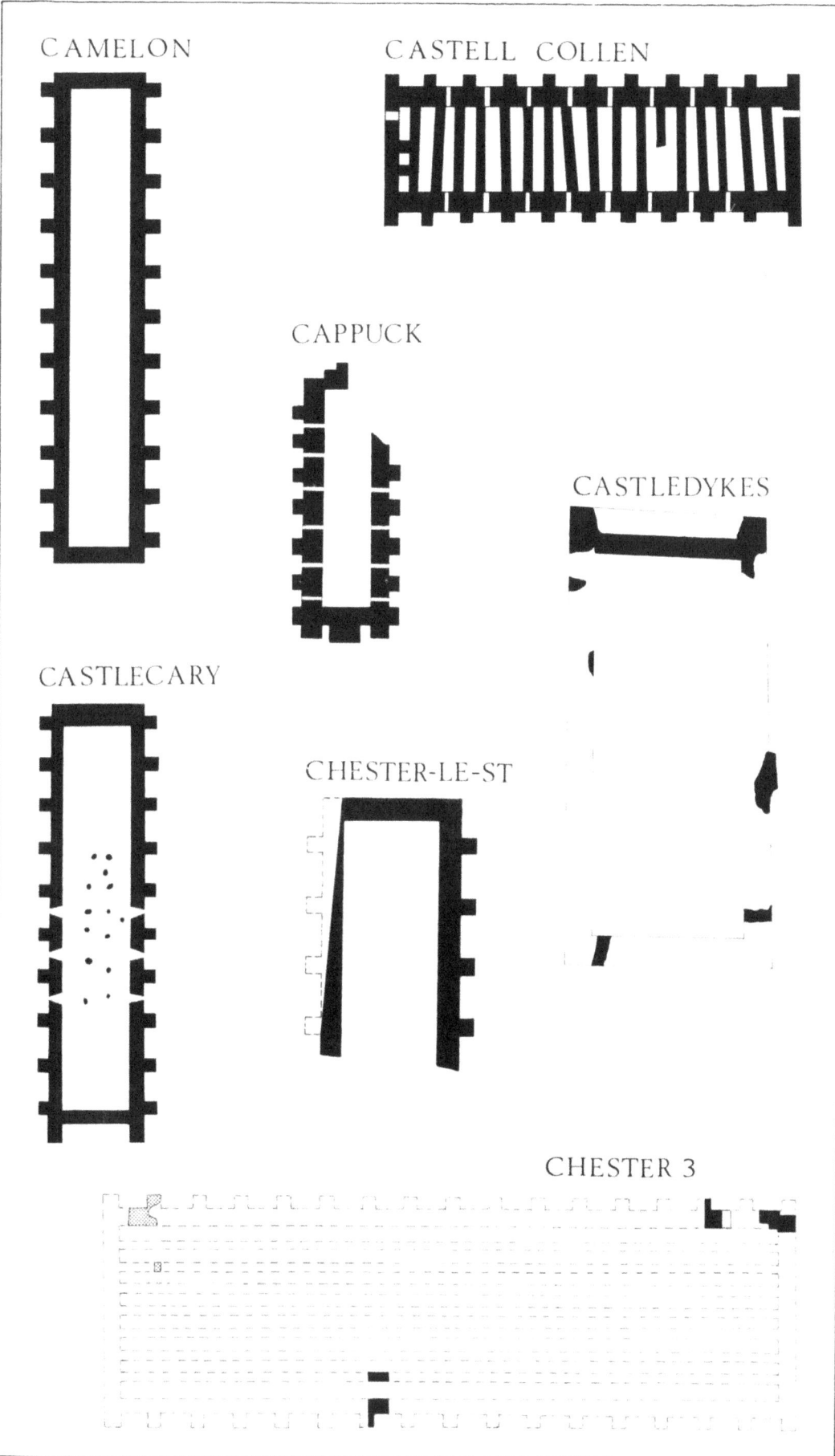

Fig. 8

CHESTER   Cheshire, SJ 4066

Overall area, 24.33 ha; 23.42 ha within ramparts.

References	Petch and Thompson, 1959.
Garrison	Legionary garrison. Legio XX Valeria Victrix from c. A.D. 88. (RIB 449 etc.).
Granaries (Fig. 8)	Four single granaries are known. Traces of one were found in 1939 and subsequently three more have been excavated more fully; it is from these examples that the following details have been compiled. All three were situated close to the porta principalis dextra, parallel with the via principalis. Early second century.

Dimensions - each 48.46 x 13.41 m overall; internally 45.82 x 11.68 m (1 and 3) and 11.37 m (2), giving a total floor area of 1591.3 sq m. Constructed with regularly coursed blocks of sandstone, mortared. The foundations consisted of grouted pebbles and sandstone rubble set in rock-cut foundation trenches. Each granary contained 7 longitudinal sleeper walls, 0.53 m thick and 0.91 m apart. The wide spacing of these walls suggests timber flooring. Only two ventilators survived; 68 and 74 cm wide respectively, parallel-sided.

A thick layer of broken roofing tiles lay between the granaries and between the sleeper walls; 6 bore the stamp LEG XX VV DE (c. A.D. 250?).

Structural alterations	No evidence for reconstruction, although the excavator suggested that the roof may have been repaired c. A.D. 250.

CHESTER-LE-STREET   Co. Durham, NZ 2750

Overall area, 2.1 ha

References	Gillam and Tait, 1968.
Garrison	Ala... Antoniniana attested A.D. 216 (RIB 1049).
Granaries (Fig. 8)	One single granary next to the east gate, at right angles to the via principalis. Construction not before the mid Antonine period.

Dimensions - the total length not ascertained, the width 9.75 m overall. The foundations consisted of heavy clay and cobbles.

CHESTERS   Northumberland, NY 9170

Overall area, 2.35 ha; 1.96 ha within ramparts.

References   Collingwood, 1933. Birley, 1960.

Granaries   In the middle of the last century John Clayton discovered and
(Fig. 10)   subsequently removed two single granaries in the retentura,
                 considering them to be late insertions. (Birley, 1961, 175).
                 The space appropriate to the granaries, next to the principia
                 in the central range, of the Hadrianic fort has not yet been
                 examined. The only plan which seems to be available is
                 published in the Handbook to the Roman Wall. However, the
                 scale is too small to permit accurate measurement of the
                 dimensions.

   Dimensions - very approx., west) 15.25 x 9.14 m overall, 13.70 x 7.20 m internally; east) 14.0 x 7.65 m overall,
   11.90 x 6.10 m internally, giving a total floor area in the
   region of 171.2 sq m.

CORBRIDGE   Northumberland, NY 9864

References   Forster and Knowles, 1909, 1910 and 1915. Forster, 1912.
VCH X 1914. Richmond and Gillam, 1950. Gillam and Tait, 1971.
Brassington, 1975; and information from Mr. J. P. Gillam.

A reappraisal of the evidence relating to the pair of granaries situated next to the west gate of the Period IVa fort, and still visible in their latest phases, has been made by Mr. J. P. Gillam, who has kindly made his notes available to me in advance of his own publication. He has elucidated four structural phases.[67]

Phase I. Part stone-part timber granaries of the Period IVa fort

Overall area, approx. 2.26 ha; approx. 1.85 ha within ramparts.

Garrison   Possibly an ala quingenaria in Period IVa, c. A.D. 139/40.
                 (Gillam and Tait, 1971, 28).

Granaries   Three single granaries. A pair of unbuttressed examples
                 underlying the later buttressed structures, between the
                 principia and the west gate, and at right angles to the via
                 principalis; and an additional one underlying the south range
                 of Site XI, parallel with the via principalis. A.D. 139/40.

(Fig. 9)   a) East and west. Dimensions of both approx. 30.0 x 10.0 m
                 overall; 28.0 x 8.0 m internally, giving a total floor area of
                 450 sq m. Traces survived only at foundation level and they
                 may be partially timbered structures erected upon masonry
                 sleeper walls, rather than entirely stone-built.[67] Unbuttres-
                 sed. The method of flooring is unknown.

   To the north of the end wall of the west granary two rectangular clay and cobble foundations 4.25 and 3.5 x 1.2 m respectively could have supported the columns of a portico.

Careful examination to the north of the east granary failed to reveal comparable evidence, and it is therefore postulated that its portico may have been situated at its southern end. The position of the portico indicates that the west granary was entered from the north, and the east granary probably from the south.

Two inscriptions, reused as paving slabs in the later granaries may relate to this period. They record building under Q. Lollius Urbicus by Legio II Augusta (RIB 1147, 1148). Mr. Gillam suggests that they might relate to the unbuttressed granaries of Phase I: it may be no coincidence that RIB 1147 was found at the north end of the west granary, and RIB 1148 at the south end of the east granary - corresponding to the position of the entrances at this period.

b) Granary, Site XI. Dimensions - 19.80 x 7.50 m overall; 18.32 x 6.02 m internally, giving a floor area of 110.3 sq m. Only two courses of masonry survived, upon foundations of clay and cobbles; this granary may also have had a timber superstructure. Unbuttressed. The floor was supported by 7 transverse sleeper walls in the eastern half, and by 2 longitudinal sleeper walls in the western part; their wide spacing suggests a timber floor.

Structural alterations
This granary was extended 7.3 m eastwards; there were no sleeper walls in the extension. The date of the modification is uncertain.

Phase 2. Modifications

A precinct wall 0.6 m wide was built enclosing the pair of unbuttressed granaries, and overlying the foundations of the portico of the west granary; whose entrance was probably reversed to the south at this time. Mr. Gillam suggests that this phase relates to occupation after the abandonment of the site as a fort, and dates the alteration to c. A.D. 162/3.

Phase 3. Earlier buttressed granaries

Probably uncompleted. The date of construction is uncertain but Mr. Gillam suggests that Site XI, the earlier period of the castellum aquae and these granaries were linked as components of a grand scheme, possibly civilian, begun in the late A.D. 170s and abandoned during the troubles of c. A.D. 180.

Dimensions - west) 29.87 x 9.14 m overall, 27,75 x 7.02 m internally; east) 28.64 x 9.75 m overall, 26.52 x 7.63 m internally, giving a total floor area of 397.1 sq m. It has been pointed out that the west granary was begun before the east,[69] for some of the footings of the east granary's buttresses overlap those of the west. There is no reason necessarily to suppose a long time lapse between them.

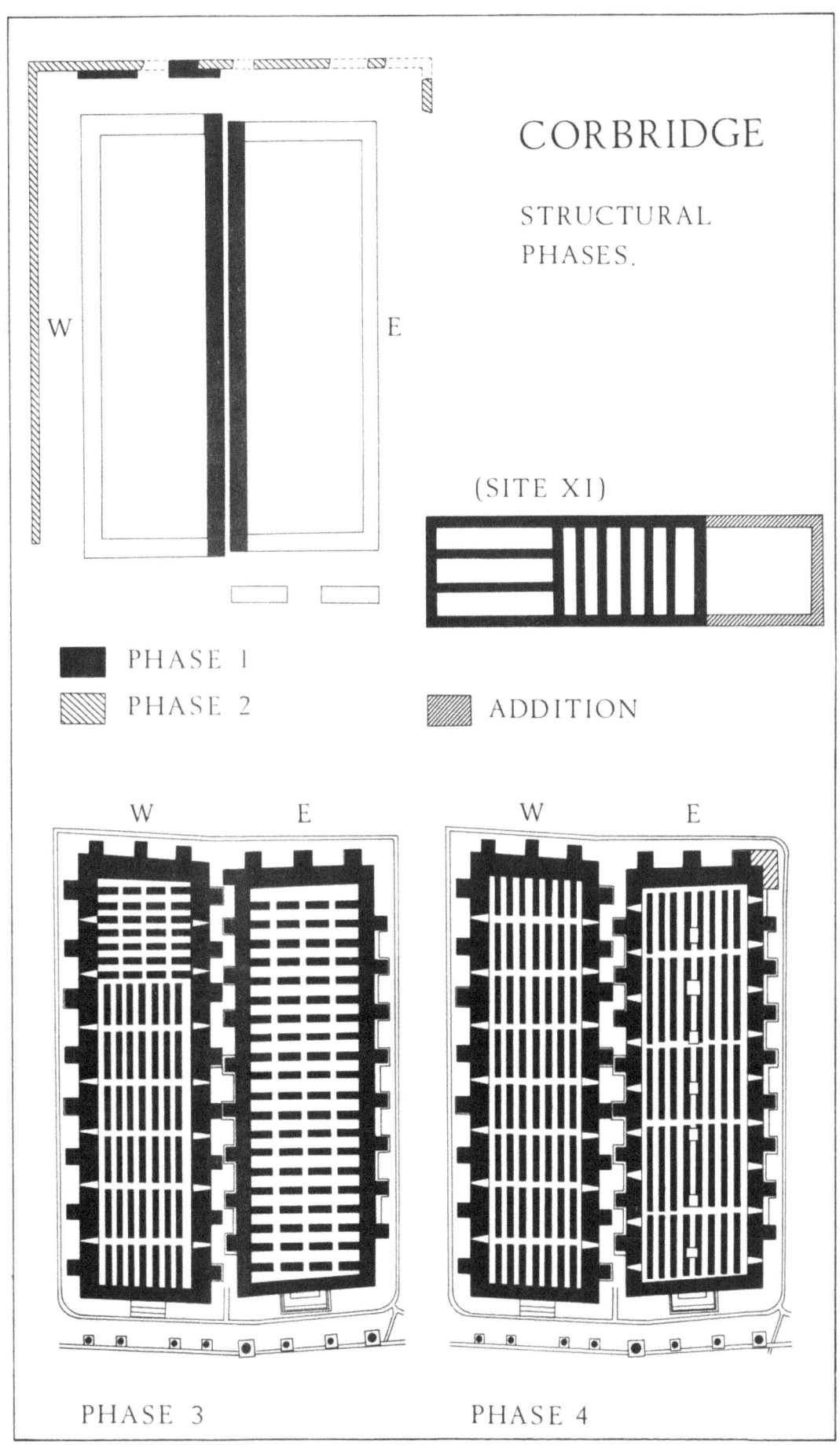

Fig. 9

a) <u>West granary</u>. Marked differences are visible between the lower 3-5 courses of shallow, rectangular masonry, roughly dressed and often ochre coloured, and the upper courses of neatly dressed square ashlar blocks. This lower level of masonry, together with the earlier of the two phases of ventilators, the lower series of sleeper walls associated with the projecting ledge inside the north wall and most of the east and west walls, represents the remains of the earlier buttressed granary. The floor was supported upon 7 rows of transverse sleeper walls in the northern quarter, and 7 rows of longitudinal sleeper walls in the remainder; 1.1 m high.

It is evident that the buttressed west granary of Phase 4 was erected upon the unfinished 3-5 courses and sleeper walls of the Phase 3 structure; the lack of demolition rubble in this phase serves to reinforce the view that this granary was under construction at the same time as Site XI, and that both projects were abandoned before completion.

b) <u>East granary</u>. It has been suggested that this structure was only erected after the complete abandonment of work on the west granary, and prior to raising the levels,[70] but Mr. Gillam cites evidence to show that work had started whilst building was taking place in the west. The lower 1-2 courses in the north, west and south walls consists of roughly dressed rectangular masonry, similar to that in the west granary. Clay and fobble foundations of at least 14 transverse walls are recorded underlying the visible longitudinal sleeper walls; they correspond with the lower sleeper walls of the adjacent granary. The presence of only a single phase of ventilators can probably be attributed to the fact that construction had commenced slightly later than its western counterpart and had not advanced quite as far when the work was abandoned.

Loading platforms 2.60 m wide were provided at the south ends of both granaries. A portico consisting of 8 columns fronted the buildings; their dimensions suggested to the excavator that they may have originally been 3.50-4.50 m high. The two central columns in each group were placed much further apart than those on the sides to enable carts to pull up to the loading platforms. The columns of the east granary were larger than those on the west; the outer ones were 0.76 m in diameter and the central ones 0.59 m whilst the western columns had a diameter of 0.50 m. A stone gutter encirlced the granaries, with a T-junction probably connecting it with an eaves-drip between the buildings; its construction predates the raising of the ground level and it seems to have continued in use, with some modifications, during both later phases of granary use.

Phase 4.   Later buttressed granaries

This phase is represented by the pair of granaries which are visible today, largely following the ground plans of their predecessors; with the same dimensions. Early third century pottery recovered from the clay and cobble packing of the earlier sleeper walls in the west granary, combined with two inscriptions, indicates a Severan date for this rebuilding. RIB 1151, from Hexham Priory records the building of a granary under L. Alfenus Senecio (A.D. 202-208); RIB 1143, from the entrance of the west granary records the 'officer in charge of the granaries at the time of the most successful expedition to Britain'; perhaps referring to the Severan campaigns of A.D. 209-11.

The walls survive to a height of 2.15 m, constructed from well dressed ashlar blocks facing a rubble core. The spaces between the sleeper walls in the west granary had been infilled with clay and cobbles to provide a base for a new series of 7 rows of longitudinal sleeper walls supporting a stone flagged floor. The east granary had 8 rows of longitudinal sleeper walls, and, in addition, 7 large pillars, of uncertain function, were constructed along the central axis of the flagged floor; it has been suggested that this was done either to strengthen a sagging roof, or to support a second storey.[71]

The ventilators of the west granary were rebuilt at a higher level, and they were present between the buttresses on the long walls of both buildings, splaying inwards; one example in the east still retains a central mullion. (Plate IIA)

Each granary possessed a stepped loading platform 4.50 m wide against its south wall (Plate IIB). The raising of levels in the vicinity of the granaries necessitated the raising of the portico columns. All four columns on the west were raised to compensate, but only the central columns on the east were raised 0.45 m; the outer ones were simply surrounded by the new road metalling. The stone drain remained in commission, with certain modifications.

Additional granaries

Excavations in 1909-13 to the north of Site XI revealed two buttressed stone buildings, of uncertain date, which may have been granaries. The eastern example (Site 56) was better preserved of the two. External dimensions - approx. 45.70 x 9.14 m. Few details are recorded, but if we assume the walls to have been 1 m thick the internal dimensions can be calculated as approx. 43.70 x 7.14 m, giving a floor area of 312.0 sq m. The increased width of the south wall may indicate the foundations of a loading platform. A drain ran in front of this building.

The possible granary to the west (Site 17) was more fragmentary. Its external width was 7 m, but its length was not ascertained. Internally there were traces of a single transverse sleeper wall.

CRAMOND	Midlothian, NT 1977

Overall area, 2.43 ha; 1.92 ha within ramparts.

References	Rae, 1959-62. Rae, A. and V. 1974.
Garrison	Probably a cohors milliaria. Coh. I Tungrorum (RIB 2135) and Coh. V Gallorum (RIB 2134) are attested.
Granaries (Fig. 10)	Two single granaries in the central range, one next to the east gate, and the other immediately to the west of the principia, both at right angles to the via principalis. Antonine.

Dimensions - total length not ascertained, east) 23.60 + x 6.70 m overall and 22.90 + x 4.50 m internally. west) 23.60 + x 5.86 m overall and 22.90 + x 4.88 m internally. Both were constructed with well dressed sandstone, the east had a damp course. The foundations consisted of rammed clay and cobbles overlain by paving 1.06-1.29 m wide. No trace of floor supports survived in the west granary, but four responds 0.76 m square for a raised floor were found at the north end of the east granary.

CRAWFORD II	Lanarkshire, NS 954214

Overall area, 0.79 ha; 0.61 ha within ramparts.

References	Maxwell, 1972.
Garrison	Possibly a vexillation of half a cohors quingenaria equitata. Four barracks in the retentura and two in the praetentura in Antonine I, with another four inferred.
Granaries (Fig. 10)	One single granary in the central range next to and south of the principia, at right angles to the via principalis. Antonine I.

Dimensions - 21.34 x 6.71 m overall; 19.52 x 4.89 m internally, giving a floor area of 95.5 sq m. Massive clay and cobble foundations.

CROY HILL	Dunbarton, NS 7276

Overall area, 0.80 ha; 0.62 ha within ramparts.

References	Macdonald, 1937.
Garrison	Probably less than a cohort.
Granaries (Fig. 10)	One single granary opposite the principia, at right angles to the via principalis. Antonine.

Dimensions - 14.12 x 5.28 m overall; 12.50 x 3.66 m internally, giving a floor area of 45.8 sq m. Shallow rock-cut foundation trenches. To traces of floor supports.

A conduit ran down the centre of the building.

Structural alterations	No provision had been made for the conduit initially, and thus a passage had to be cut through the north wall.
DONCASTER	South Yorkshire, SE 5703

Overall area, 2.6 ha

References	Buckland and Dolby, 1972 and 1973.
Granaries	Excavations on a construction site east of St. George Gate revealed two large stone buildings thought to be granaries of Hadrianic date. They were situated close to the south gate of the fort.
DOVER	Kent, TR 3141
References	Philp, 1971, 1972 and 1973.
Granaries	Excavations in 1970 revealed a second century <u>Classis Britannica</u> fort underlying the Saxon Shore fort. A large proportion of the interior was examined, and parts of at least three granaries were recorded. One example, in the Queen St. area, stood to a height of 1.85 m and another, in the Durham Hill area, 2.75 m high. A beam slot and soffits were found half way up the interior wall of this building, suggesting to the excavator that this granary may have had a second storey. The site is not yet fully published, and it has proved impossible to obtain further details from the excavator.
DRUMBURGH	Cumbria, NY 2659

Overall area, 0.8 ha.

References	Haverfield, 1899. Simpson and Richmond, 1952.
Garrison	Possibly too small for a full cohort.
Granaries (Fig. 10)	Fragmentary remains of the north-west corner of a granary were found inside the north-west angle of the fort, between the west wall of the fort and Hadrian's Wall, leaving insufficient space for a rampart or an intervallum road. <u>c</u>. A.D. 160.

The dimensions are unknown. Constructed with a mortared rubble core faced with thin sandstone slabs upon foundations consisting of a few cobbles in red clay. No traces of floor supports are known. One ventilator remained close to the north-west corner, which splayed from 18-35 cm inwards.

A quantity of 'black matter' was found outside the ventilator.

GELLIGAER II   Mid Glamorgan, ST 1397

Overall area, 1.49 ha; 1.15 ha within ramparts.

References	Ward, 1903.
Garrison	Probably a <u>cohors quingenaria equitata</u>. Three pairs of barracks located. Building IV has been suggested as accommodation for two turmae, and Building IX as stabling. (Breeze and Dobson, 1969, 18).
Granaries (Fig. 10)	Two single granaries in the central range, next to the east and west gates respectively, at right angles to the via principalis. Trajanic.

Dimensions - both 18.29 x 8.80 m overall; 16.15 x 7.01 m internally, giving a total floor area of 226.4 sq.m. The buttresses and side walls were founded on stone rafts. The floors were supported upon transverse sleeper walls; the east granary had 6 and the west 8, reduced to 5, with central openings 0.91 m wide. The west granary had a rough stone floor upon which the transverse walls were erected. The wide spacing of the sleeper walls suggests timber flooring. Ventilators were placed between the buttresses on the long walls; originally 1.22 m wide, reduced to 0.91 m.

Loading platforms were provided at each end of both granaries, 2.89 m wide, projecting 1.83-2.13 m. The possible position of porticos was suggested by the excavator from examination of worn and unworn flagstones on the loading platforms. Drains ran parallel with the east side of the east granary, and in front of both. Large quantities of red roofing tiles were recovered.

Structural alterations	Reduction of 8 transverse walls to 5 in the west granary and the fact that the 5 existing buttresses were secondary indicated modifications.

GREAT CHESTERS   Northumberland, NY 7066

Overall area, 1.4 ha.

References	Gibson, 1903.
Garrison	<u>RIB</u> 1738 records the restoration from ground level of a granary, fallen into decay through old age, by Coh. II Asturum; dated A.D. 225. However, the date of the extant granary is unknown.
Granaries (Fig. 11)	Fragments of a single granary were found next to the west gate, parallel with the via principalis. Date unknown.

Maximum recorded length - 17.37 m, and overall breadth - 6.50 m. The floor was supported upon transverse sleeper walls 0.91 m wide; the method of flooring is unknown.

A quantity of charred wheat was recovered from the interior.

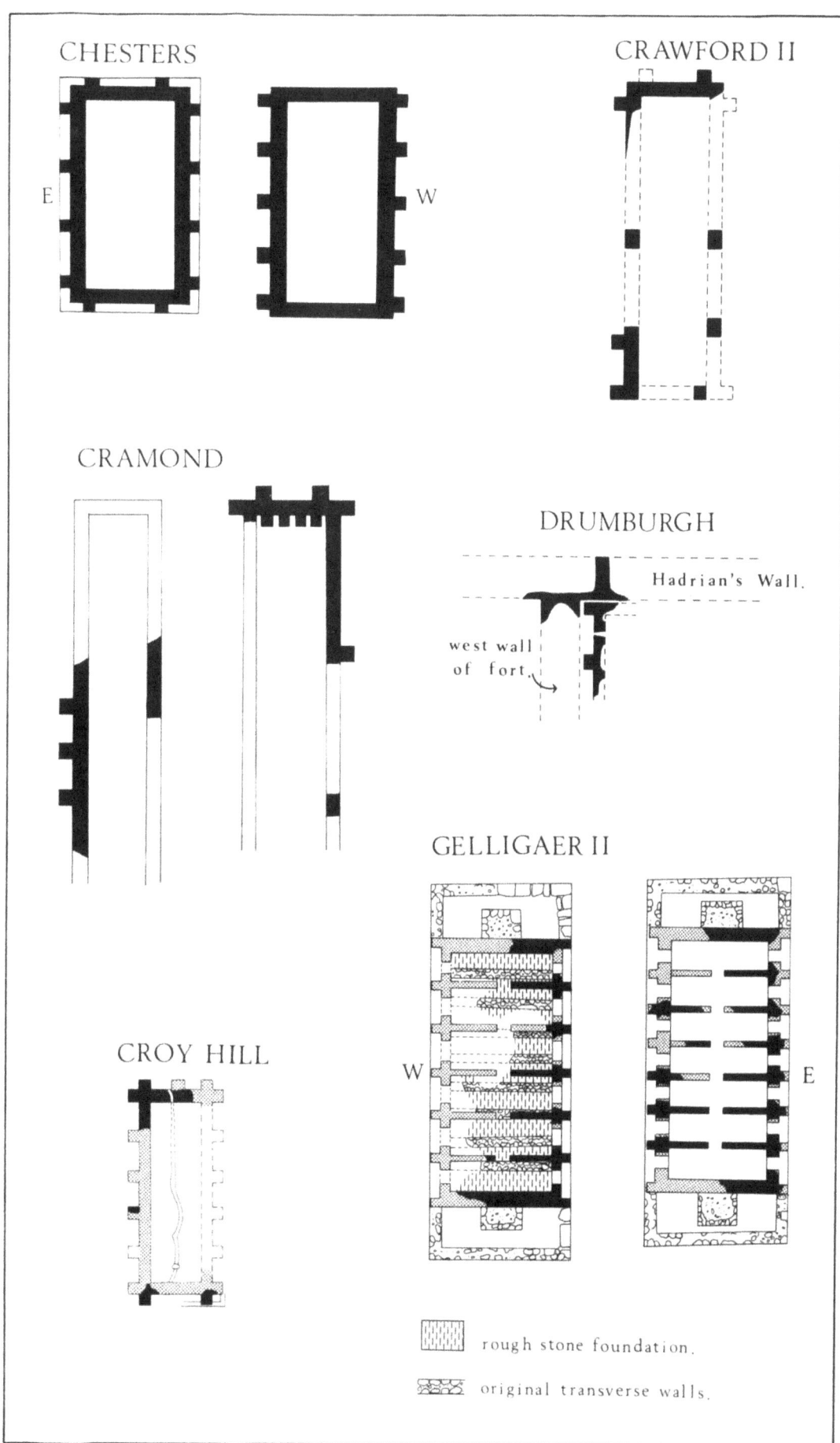

Fig. 10

HALTONCHESTERS   Northumberland, NY 9968

Overall area, 1.75 ha, although later enlarged to 1.96 ha; 1.48 ha within ramparts.

References	Gillam, 1961a, 1961b and 1962. (interim notes).
Garrison	Probably a <u>cohors quingenaria equitata</u> originally.
Granaries	One single granary in the central range, west of the principia. Hadrianic.

> Dimensions - 41.15 x 10.36 m overall. If we assume the walls to be of the same thickness as the majority of other examples, 1 m, the floor area available would be, very approximately, 330 sq m. The foundations consisted of a massive stone raft of flagging set in clay, underlying the whole building. In the north part the cross walls supporting the floor ran north-south; whilst in the southern part they ran east-west. They appeared contemporary. Traces of a wooden floor were detected plus a quantity of grain which had stood upon it and had become charred during the late third century destruction of the building.
>
> Sandstone roofing material was associated with the granary.

HALTWHISTLE BURN   Northumberland, NY 7166

Overall area 0.32 ha; 0.28 ha within ramparts.

References	Gibson and Simpson, 1909.
Garrison	This fortlet too small for a full cohort. One barrack block excavated.
Granaries (Fig. 11)	One single granary next to the south gate, at right angles to the via principalis. Hadrianic.

> Dimensions - 11.96 x 9.15 m overall; 10.74 x 7.93 m internally, giving a floor area of 85.2 sq m. Constructed with rough sandstone upon foundations of cobblestones. The method of floor support and flooring is unknown.
>
> Three quarters of all the vessels from the fortlet were found inside and around this granary.

HARDKNOTT   Cumbria, NY 2101

Overall area, 1.31 ha; 1.07 ha within ramparts.

References	Collingwood, 1928. Charlesworth, 1963.
Garrison	Probably a <u>cohors quingenaria</u>. Coh. IIII Delmatorum is attested under Hadrian. (<u>JRS</u> 55 1965, 222 no. 7).
Granaries (Fig. 11)	One double granary in the central range to the north-east of the principia, at right angles to the via principalis. Hadrianic.

Dimensions - 16.45 x 13.48 m overall; ne) 14.33 x 5.49 m (reduced to 4.27 m) internally. sw) 14.33 x 5.18 m internally, giving a total floor area of 135.4 sq m. There were 7 central piers in each granary to support the floor; there may also have been a sleeper wall between some of the piers, removed by the 1928 excavation. The spacing of the piers implies a timber floor.

Loading platforms were provided against the south east wall of each granary; the sw being better preserved, faced with roughly dressed stones and rubble-filled. To the west of the loading platform in the sw granary was a small opening to the east of the loading platform in the ne part. The walls of the sw granary had been plastered.
ing only 0.60 m wide, later blocked; and a similar opening to the east of the loading platform in the n.e. part. The walls of the sw granary had been plastered.

Structural alterations	The granary had originally a single partition, but later a second wall was added in the ne part of the building, but was not bonded in.

HIGH ROCHESTER   Northumberland, NY 8398

Overall area, 2.01 ha; 1.70 ha within ramparts.

References	Bruce, 1857. Richmond, 1940.
Garrison	Possibly a <u>cohors quingenaria</u> replaced by a <u>cohors milliaria equitata</u> in the third century. Coh. I Lingonum equitata is attested in the Antonine period under Q. Lollius Urbicus A.D. 139-43. (<u>RIB</u> 1276).
Granaries (Fig. 11)	Two double granaries. Excavation revealed a double granary in the central range immediately to the west of the principia. Although the building on the east side of the principia was not fully uncovered the excavator felt that it had been examined in sufficient detail to be able to postulate an identical structure to that on the west. Both pairs at right angles to the via principalis. Antonine.

Dimensions are approx. because taken from a small scale plan. All 4 - 23.15 x 6.40 m overall; 21.0 x 4.27 m internally, giving a total floor area of 359.2 sq m. Longitudinal sleeper walls were located in all the granaries, although the type of flooring is unknown. Ventilators were present between the buttresses on the long walls.

Entrances were located at the north end of each granary, providing access to the via principalis.

HOUSESTEADS   Northumberland, NY 7968

Overall area, 2.10 ha; 1.73 ha within ramparts.

References	Bosanquet, 1904. Ministry of Works, 1952.
Garrison	Probably a <u>cohors milliaria peditata</u> under Hadrian. No Hadrianic garrison attested. Ten barrack blocks excavated, containing 10-11 contubernia.
Granaries (Fig. 11)	One double granary in the central range next to and north of the principia, at right angles to the via principalis. Hadrianic.

Dimensions - 25.60 x 14.50 m overall; each half 23.78 x 5.49 m internally, giving a total floor area of 261.1 sq m. The floor of the north granary was supported upon 5 rows of stone pillars (Plate IIIA and B). There is some divergence between published plans as to the floor supports of the southern half. The original excavator stated that longitudinal sleeper walls were present. However, the plan published in the Guidebook[72] shows pillars in the se part and longitudinal walls in the nw. Observation of the extant remains suggests that both halves of the south granary may have originally contained pillars; the height of the ventilators and the projecting ledge upon which the timber floor would have rested, suggests that the stone blocks were used upright as pillars, rather than laid on their sides in rows of parallel longitudinal walls. Projecting ledges ran along the interior of the central walls to support timber floor joists; sockets were provided in the walls to locate them.

Both granaries were entered by flights of steps at the west end, leading to an open space at the rear of the building.

Structural alterations: It has been suggested that the piers running down the centre of the entire building between the two partition walls represent the original roof supports, and that first one and then a second partition was added to replace them.[73] In the final stages of the fort's occupation the granaries were converted into living accommodation; the spaces between the floor supports being filled in and flagged over. Subsequently a conical corn drying kiln was inserted in the centre of the south granary. Its date is uncertain, but Professor Birley believes that it can be attributed to the period of occupation by the 'Moss Troopers' in the reign of Elizabeth I.[74]

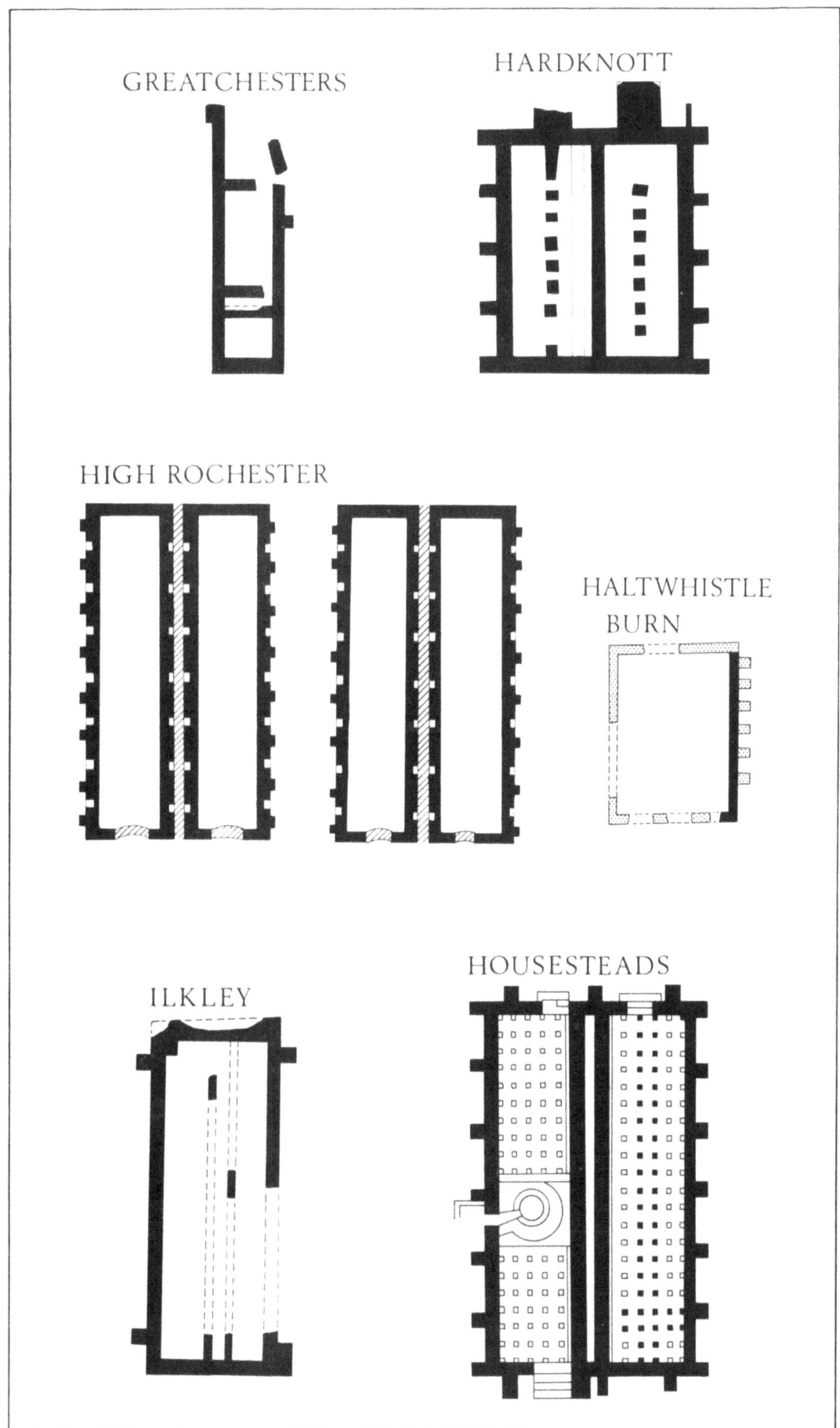

Fig.11

ILKLEY	West Yorkshire, SE 1148

Overall area, 0.97 ha; 0.70 ha within ramparts.

References	Woodward, 1926. Hartley, 1966.
Garrison	Possibly a cohors quingenaria. Infantry cohorts are attested, RIB 635 Coh II Lingonum, and RIB 636, dated A.D. 161-9.
Granaries (Fig. 11)	One single granary in the central range next to, and north of the principia, at right angles to the via principalis. Uncertain date.
	Dimensions - 23.77 x 9.14 m overall; 21.79 x 7.01 m internally, giving a floor area of 152.8 sq m. Foundations consisted of cobble and rough stone. Two longitudinal sleeper walls probably supported a timber floor (a quantity of nails found).
	A possible loading platform at the east end was represented by a mass of stones rammed tightly and extending to the edge of the via principalis. Debris associated with this granary included numerous fragments of burnt wood, charred wheat, many nails and a large number of amphora fragments; numerous thin slabs of white or yellow freestone may represent roofing material.
INVERESK	Midlothian, NT 3472
References	Richmond, 1947 and 1948.
Granaries	Excavations in 1946-7 in St. Michael's Garden revealed barrack blocks and a stable overlying the se corner of a buttressed granary, associated with Antonine pottery. A second granary was located within a transverse block of buildings examined in the cemetery.
LANCASTER	Lancashire, SD 4762
References	Richmond, 1959.
Granaries	Excavations in 1958 in the Vicarage Field Allotments revealed the foundations of a stone granary. The walling had been almost completely robbed, and only fragmentary traces of sleeper walls survived.
LYNE	Peebles, NT 1840

Overall area, 2.61 ha; 2.24 ha within ramparts.

References	Christison, 1901. H.M.S.O. 1967.
Garrison	Possibly a cohors milliaria. No garrison is attested.
Granaries (Fig. 12)	One single and one double granary in the central range on either side of the principia, at right angles to the via principalis. c. A.D. 158.

Dimensions - single) 29.56 x 6.10 m overall, 27.43 x 3.96 m internally; double) 29.26 x 30.48 m overall, northern part - 27.43 x 12.19 m internally and southern, 27.43 x 15.24 m internally, giving the total floor area of both granaries of 861.0 sq m. Both were constructed with red sandstone ashlar blocks on foundations of blue whinstone bedded in clay. Three transverse sleeper walls survived in the single granary, and two longitudinal sleeper walls in the double.

MUMRILLS   Stirling, NS 9179

Overall area, 2.86 ha; 2.64 ha within ramparts.

References   Macdonald and Curle, 1928. Breeze and Dobson, 1973, 116.

Garrison   Original Antonine garrison probably an ala quingenaria, RIB 2140 records Ala II Tungrorum. Subsequently replaced in Antonine II by a cohors quingenaria equitata, cf. RIB 2142 which attests Coh II Thracum.

Granaries   Two single granaries in the central range on either side of
(Fig. 12)   the principia, at right angles to the via principalis. Antonine.

Dimensions - east) 30.07 x 6.55 m overall, 27.63 x 4.11 m internally; west) 30.02 x 6.91 m overall, 27.58 x 4.47 m internally, giving a total floor area of 236.8 sq m. Foundations consisted of boulders set in clay. The floor was supported upon three longitudinal sleeper walls 0.47 m wide in each granary. One ventilator remained; splaying inwards from 17-25 cm.

The possible foundations of a loading platform were located between the 2nd and 3rd buttresses from the north in the west granary.

NEWSTEAD   Roxburgh, NT 5734

Overall area, 6.2 ha; 5.4 ha within ramparts.

References   Curle, 1911. Richmond, 1950. Breeze and Dobson, 1969, 22.

Garrison   Possibly a two cohort detachment of Legio XX and an ala quingenaria in the Antonine I fort. Legio XX is attested (RIB 2120, 2122-4, 2127), and a decurion of Ala Augusta Vocontiorum (RIB 2121). 12 barrack blocks in the praetentura, with stabling in the retentura. The Antonine II garrison may have been an ala milliaria.

Granaries   Two single granaries in the central range on either side of the
(Fig. 12)   principia, at right angles to the via principalis. Antonine.

Dimensions - north) 40.0 x 12.0 m overall, 38.48 x 10.48 m internally; south) 38.5 x 11.0 m overall, 36.98 x 9.48 m internally, giving a total floor area of 753.8 sq m. The north granary was constructed from sandstone, blue greywacke, reused brick and quern fragments; the south with red sandstone ashlar. Both had heavy cobble foundations, carried to the external face of the buttresses. In both the floor was supported upon longitudinal sleeper walls 0.43 m wide.

The remains of a loading platform 3.05 m long and 35 cm high survived against the west wall of the south granary. Near the south west corner of this granary, 0.65 m from the wall was a column with a circular base, possibly the remains of a portico.

On the opposite side of the via principalis was a long, narrow building with irregularly spaced transverse sleeper walls; it has been thought that this structure may have housed animal fodder.

Structural alterations: The walls of the north granary contained much reused material which suggests rebuilding.

OLD CHURCH, BRAMPTON   Cumbria, NY 5061

Overall area, 1.52 ha; 1.27 ha within ramparts.

References: Simpson and Richmond, 1936.

Garrison: Unknown.

Granaries (Fig. 13): Two single granaries at either end of the central range, next to the east and west gates respectively, at right angles to the via principalis. Possibly Hadrianic.

Dimensions - east) 23.16 x 7.92 m overall, 21.34 x 6.10 m internally; west) 25.29 x 7.92 m overall, 23.47 x 6.10 m internally, giving a total floor area of 273.3 sq m. The west granary was constructed upon a broad flagged foundation, whilst the east was built upon flags following the line of the buttresses. In both granaries longitudinal sleeper walls supported the floor. Ventilators were present between the buttresses on the long walls.

OLD KILPATRICK   Dunbarton, NS 4673

Overall area, 1.91 ha; 1.68 ha within ramparts.

References: Miller, 1928. Breeze and Dobson, 1973, 120.

Garrison: The excavator suggested that the original Antonine garrison was a cohors milliaria, perhaps reduced to a cohors quingenaria peditata in Antonine II; Coh. I Baetasiorum is attested (Brit. I 1970, 310 no. 20). Six timber barracks are recorded in the praetentura, with room for a further four in the retentura.

Granaries (Fig. 13): One single granary in the central range next to and north of the principia, at right angles to the via principalis. Antonine.

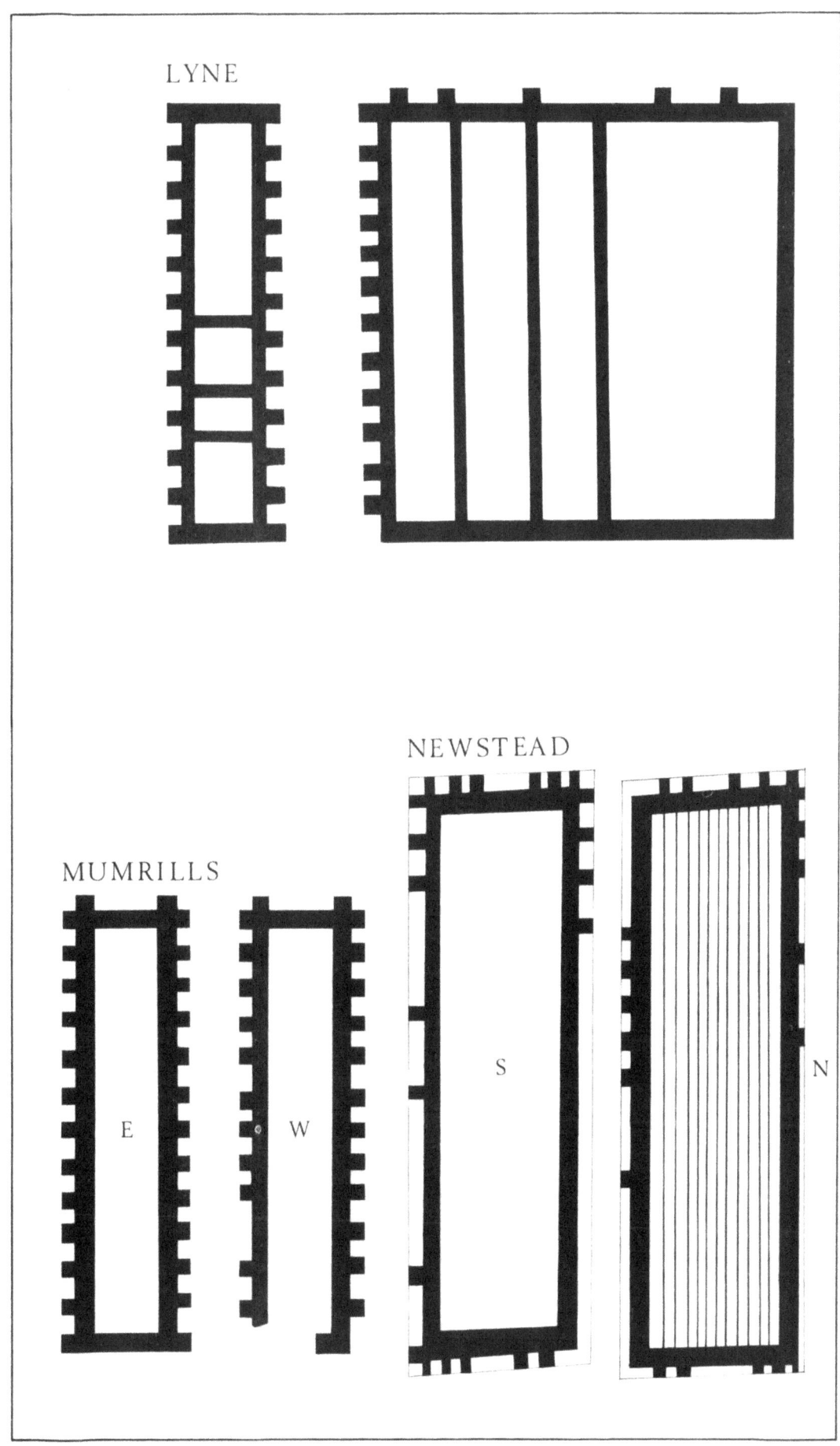

Fig. 12

Dimensions - 26.20 x 7.61 m overall; 24.08 x 5.49 m internally, giving a floor area of 132.2 sq m. Only the clay and cobble foundations of the external walls survived, together with two small patches of foundations for longitudinal sleeper walls.

Parallel to the south wall a row of cobbling 1.50 m broad, extending to within 3.60 m of the east end are thought to have been connected with a loading bay.

On the opposite side of the principia were three post-built structures at right angles to the via principalis. The most northerly of these, adjacent to the principia probably represents a timber granary contemporary with the stone granary.[75] Its dimensions - 25.91 x 6.10 m giving a floor area of approx. 158 sq m

OLD PENRITH   Cumbria, NY 4938

References   St. Joseph, 1951, 54.

Granaries   Aerial photography has located two granaries in the central range of stone buildings, to the east of the principia.

PENYDARREN   Mid Glamorgan, SO 0506

Overall area, 2 ha, although the actual extent is unknown.

References   James, 1906.

Granaries (Fig. 13)   Traces of one single granary surviving; the internal layout of the fort is unknown. Possibly Trajanic.

Dimensions - only 18.30 m length remaining x 10.66 m overall width. Constructed of quarry hewn stone and mortared. At least 10 transverse sleeper walls approx. 0.45 m wide remained; three with central openings. A projecting ledge ran around the interior walls to support the floor which, judging from the quantity of nails retrieved from between the sleeper walls, was timber.

PUMPSAINT   Dyfed, SN 658401

Overall area, 1.9 ha.

References   Jones and Little, 1973.

Granaries   Traces of one granary in the central range parallel with the via principalis. Late Flavian-Trajanic.

Full dimensions are unknown. Four longitudinal sleeper walls approx. 0.70 m wide and approx 2 m apart supported the floor; their wide spacing implies a timber floor. Massive postholes were located along the inner face of the external wall, and also parallel with one of the sleeper walls, at 1.25 m intervals. The excavator has suggested that they represent a timber frame which either served to tie the roof beams, or to support a timber floor.[76]

A drain ran parallel with the west wall.

RIBCHESTER Lancashire, SD 6535

Overall area, c. 2.51 ha; 2.04 ha within ramparts.

References	Hopkinson, 1928. Hartley, 1958.
Garrison	RIB 583 records a numerus equitum Sarmatarum, and RIB 586, Coh II Asturum.
Granaries (Fig. 13)	Two single granaries in the central range between the principia and the north gate, at right angles to the via principalis. Date uncertain.

Dimensions - north) 31.39 x 7.01 m overall, 29.87 x 5.49 m internally; south) 31.39 x 6.55 m overall, 29.87 x 5.03 m, internally giving a total floor area of 314.2 sq m. The north granary contained a central longitudinal sleeper wall; charred wood suggests a timber floor. The south granary had 2 rows of upright sandstone blocks, roughly squared on a squared base, 1.50 m apart and 0.76 m from the side walls. A projecting ledge 1 m high ran round the interior to support the stone flagged floor. Ventilators were present between the buttresses on the long walls.

A well worn door sill was located at the east end of the south granary. Both had loading platforms at their eastern ends, with clay and cobble foundations. A gutter ran in front of the buildings, parallel with the via principalis. A layer of charred corn varying in depth from 0.1-0.6 m was discovered in the north granary; and a smaller quantity of charred grain in the south.

Structural alterations: Consolidation for the D.O.E. in 1957,[77] found that the space occupied by the south granary had once been an open courtyard between two large stone granaries. No dating evidence recovered.

ROUGH CASTLE Stirling, NS 8479

Overall area, 0.66 ha; 0.42 ha within ramparts.

References	Buchanan, 1905.
Garrison	Coh. VI Nerviorum is attested (RIB 2144, 2145), but the fortlet is too small for a full cohort.
Granaries (Fig. 14)	One single granary in the central range between the principia and the praetorium, at right angles to the via principalis. Presumably built c. A.D. 140.

Dimensions - 22.09 x 6.24 m overall; 20.57 x 4.72 m internally, giving a floor area of 97.1 sq m. A flagged floor was supported upon longitudinal sleeper walls 0.40 m wide;

the floor was carried through the walls and buttresses as a bonding course. Ventilators 22 x 12 cm occurred between the buttresses on the long walls.

Two steps led up to a loading platform at the north end consisting of flagstones bedded on rough-built stone supports 1.06 m wide, projecting 0.52 m.

The space between the granary and principia was closed by a connecting wall, pierced to allow the passage of a drain parallel with the east wall.

RUDCHESTER Northumberland, NZ 1167

Overall area, 1.85 ha; 1.51 ha within ramparts.

References	Brewis, 1924. Breeze and Dobson, 1974, 17.
Garrison	Possibly a cohors quingenaria equitata. A barrack, perhaps to house cavalry was located in 1972. (Brit. IV 1973, 276).
Granaries (Fig. 13)	One single granary in the central range, next to and north west of the principia, at right angles to the via principalis. Hadrianic.

Dimensions - exact length not ascertained, but estimated as 37.32 x 9.13 m overall; 35.20 x 7.01 m internally, giving a floor area of 246.8 sq m.

A massive masonry platform 9.75 x 3.05 m was located at the sw end, and an identical structure was postulated by the excavator at the opposite end.

SLACK West Yorkshire, SE 0817

Overall area, 1.5 ha; approx 1.3 ha within ramparts.

References	Dodd and Woodward, 1923. Hartley, K. F., 1972.
Garrison	Tiles bearing the stamp COH IIII BRE (Breucorum).
Granaries (Fig. 14)	One double granary in the central range between the principia and the nw gate, at right angles to the via principalis. Uncertain date.

Dimensions - 19.81 x 13.41 m overall; each half 17.98 x 5.33 m internally, giving a total floor area of 191.7 sq m. Constructed with undressed and uncoursed stones laid in puddled clay foundations. Ventilators were placed at regular intervals of 1.37 m on the long walls, splaying inwards from 15-61 cm. Unbuttressed.

Each half had an entrance 0.91 m wide in its west wall; at the entrance to the southern part was a step 0.45 m broad consisting of 2 courses of stone overlying a layer of red tiles. At the front of the granary, on the east side was a rough pavement of irregular flags which may have served as a loading area. A large quantity of roofing tiles was associated with this building.

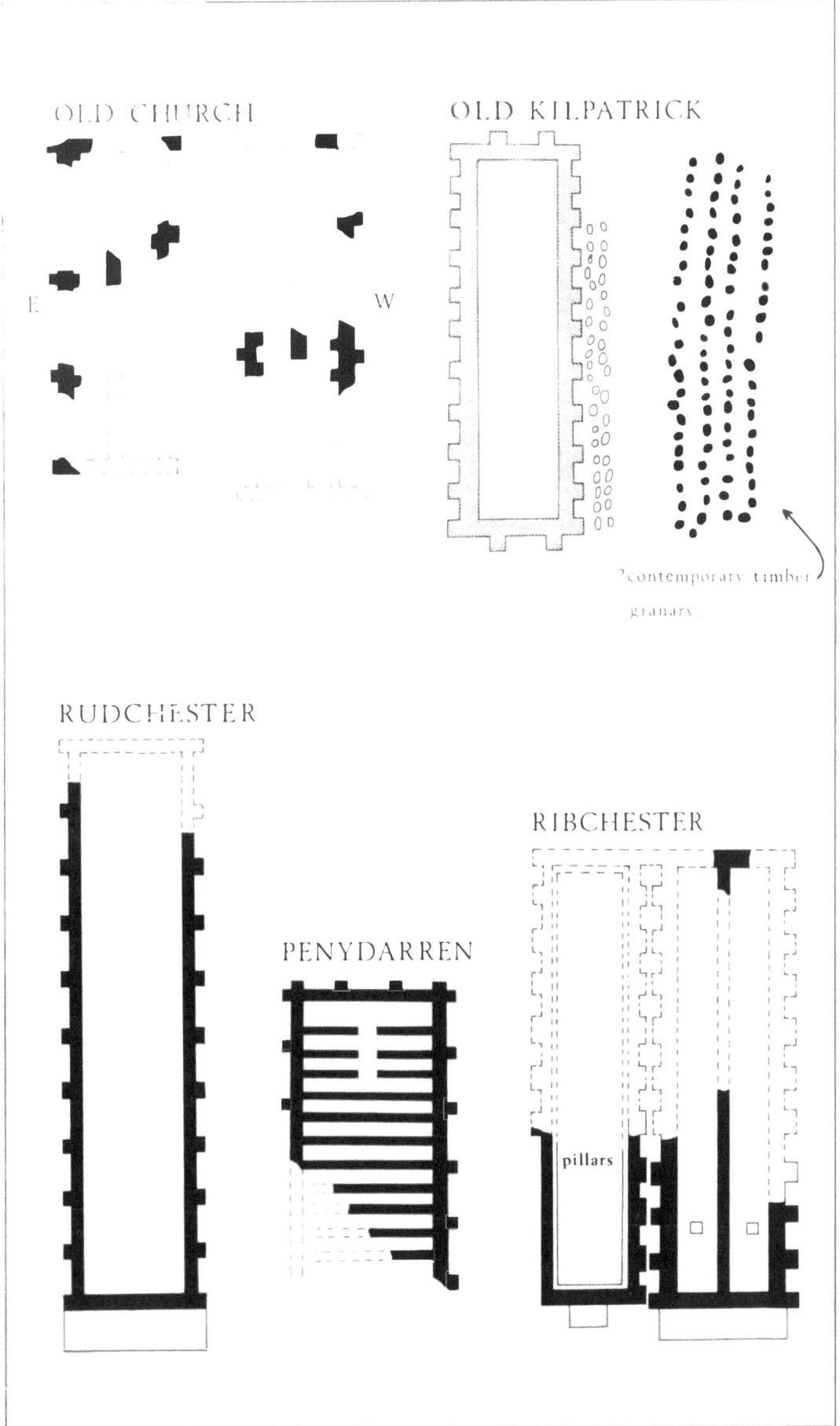

Fig. 13

SOUTH SHIELDS   Tyne and Wear. NZ 3667

Overall area, 2.09 ha; 1.73 ha within ramparts.

References	Richmond, 1934. Gillam, 1967. Breeze, 1968.
Garrison	Possibly an <u>ala quingenaria</u> under Hadrian; 6 timber barracks /stables in praetentura. 1 double-ended barrack in retentura. Coh. V Gallorum attested by RIB 1059, 1060, and several Severan lead seals; and also recorded at Cramond at unknown date (RIB 2134). Possibly this unit occupied both forts simultaneously in Severan period (Breeze, 1968). Only 2 Severan barracks excavated and 2 inferred in most southerly third of retentura.
Granaries (Fig. 14)	a) <u>Hadrianic.</u> One double granary in the central range next to the SW gate, at right angles to the via principalis.

Dimensions - 22.86 x 15.24 m overall; 20.42 x 6.10 (north part) and 6.70 m (south) internally, giving a total floor area of 261.4 sq m. Constructed with re-used blocks of grit mingled with magnesian limestone. Four rows of stone piers in each half of the building supported a stone flagged floor. Ventilators were present between the buttresses on the long walls.

Three chamfered bases with squared blocks of the portico survived in front of the building.

(Fig. 3)   b) <u>Severan.</u> 18 single granaries (2 more inferred), built in three parallel rows occupying the praetentura, the central range, and half of the retentura, at right angles to the via principalis. The Hadrianic double granary remained in use.

Several granaries, the double and nine singles were excavated in 1875 and published fully by Richmond.[78] Recent excavations in 1966 added considerably to the number known, and also modified the dimensions shown on Richmond's plan. The final report is not yet published, - therefore all dimensions given are taken from an interim plan which is too small to enable accurate measurement; those given below are approximations.

Dimensions: i) 4 singles in central range: 27.42 x 6.10 m overall, 25.42 x 4.10 m internally, giving a total floor area of 416.9 sq m. ii) 14 singles in praetentura and retentura: 29.89 x 6.10 m overall, 27.87 x 4.10 m internally, giving a total floor area of 1828.3 sq m. The total floor area available for storage during the Severan period would have been 2506.5 sq m.

All the single granaries were constructed with Gateshead Fell sandstone. Longitudinal sleeper walls, were interrupted at intervals to correspond with ventilators in the long walls; floors were flagged.

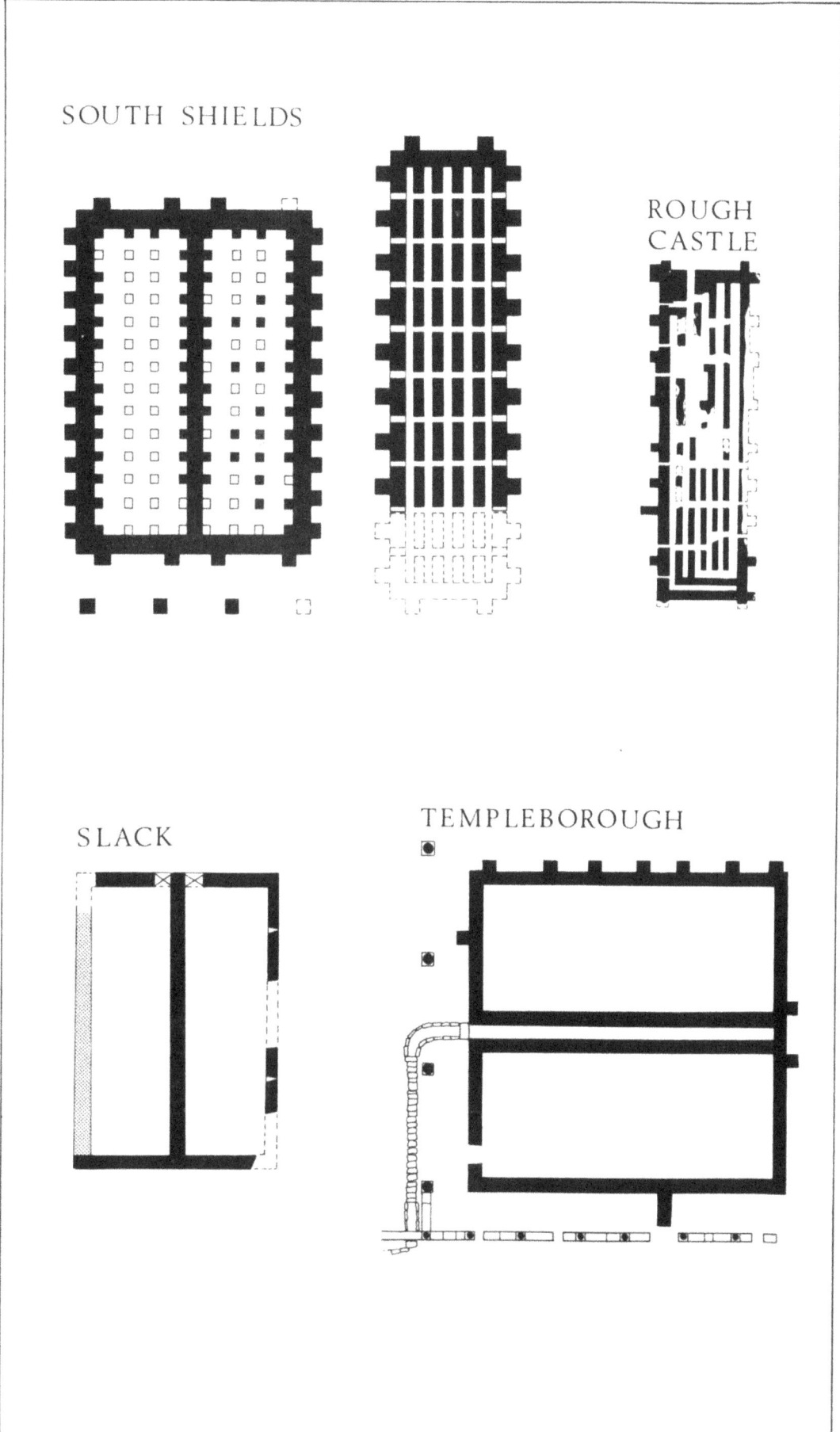

Fig. 14

The nw walls of the granaries in the retentura had been thickened, probably to form loading platforms. Thirty lead seals discovered in the fort; half bearing the heads of Severus and his sons AVGG (A.D. 198-209), and 7 of the remainder stamped by Coh V Gallorum;[79] probably originally attached to official stores.

Structural alterations
Subsequently ventilators were blocked, floor channels infilled and rooms added internally to provide living accommodation.

STANWIX   Cumbria, NY 4057

Overall area, 3.77 ha; 3.65 ha within ramparts.

References   Richmond, 1941.

Garrison   Probably the only fort on Hadrian's Wall large enough to house the ala Petriana.[80]

Granaries   One single granary within the praetentura, in the nw quarter of the fort, parallel with the via principalis. Possibly Hadrianic.

Estimated dimensions - 36.58 x 9.14 m overall; 34.76 x 7.32 m internally, giving a floor area of approx. 254.4 sq m.

TEMPLEBOROUGH   South Yorkshire, SK 4191

Overall area approx. 1.83 ha; 1.37 ha within ramparts.

References   May, 1922.

Garrison   Possibly a cohors milliaria, 10 timber barracks recorded; 2 rebuilt in stone. Coh. IIII Gallorum is attested. (RIB 619, 620).

Granaries (Fig. 14)
One double granary in the central range between the principia and the se gate, parallel with the via principalis. Date uncertain, probably c. A.D. 100.[82]

Dimensions - 21.03 x 22.02 m overall; each half 19.21 x 8.30 m internally, giving a total floor area of 318.9 sq m. Constructed with square faced sandstone rubble on clay and cobble foundations. The compacted yellow clay floor was overlain by hearths.

A possible entrance on the south side of the east granary. Four columns on the south side, and seven on the east probably supported a verandah. A flagged drain ran between the two buildings and drained away towards the se gate.

Structural alterations
A compartment 4.27 m square was constructed in the west granary.

WATERCROOK   Cumbria, SD 5190

References   St.Joseph, 1951, 54.

Granaries   The principia and two granaries have been located by aerial photography.

WHITLEY CASTLE   Northumberland, NY 6948

References   Shaw et al., 1958.

Granaries   Excavations in 1957 revealed an unbuttressed stone granary sealing pottery of the later second century.

PLATE IA. Corbridge: west granary.

PLATE IB. Corbridge (west). Longitudinal sleeper walls supporting flagged floor.

PLATE IIA.

Corbridge (east). Ventilator with central mullion.

PLATE IIB.   Corbridge (east).   Loading platform, portico column and drain.

PLATE IIIA. Housesteads (north). Pillar floor supports.

PLATE IIIB. Housesteads (north). Relationship of ventilator to floor supports.

www.ingramcontent.com/pod-product-compliance
Lightning Source LLC
Chambersburg PA
CBHW061543010526
44113CB00023B/2782